MAX AXIOM
AND THE SOCIETY OF SUPER SCIENTISTS

LIVING AMONG ROBOTS

BY *AILYNN COLLINS*
ILLUSTRATED BY *EDUARDO GARCIA*

CAPSTONE PRESS
a capstone imprint

T0011300

Published by Capstone Press, an imprint of Capstone
1710 Roe Crest Drive
North Mankato, Minnesota 56003
capstonepub.com

Copyright © 2024 by Capstone. All rights reserved. No part of this publication may be reproduced in whole or in part, or stored in a retrieval system, or transmitted in any form or by any means, electronic, mechanical, photocopying, recording, or otherwise, without written permission of the publisher.

Library of Congress Cataloging-in-Publication Data
Names: Collins, Ailynn, 1964– author.
Title: Living among robots / by Ailynn Collins.
Description: North Mankato, Minnesota : Capstone Press, an imprint of Capstone, [2024] | Series: A Max Axiom super scientist adventure | Includes bibliographical references. | Audience: Ages 8 to 11 | Audience: Grades 4-6
Summary: "When someone mentions the word "robot," what comes to mind? Many people think of mechanical characters often seen in science fiction films. But look around and you'll notice that our world is full of robots. From medical devices people use to help them walk to probes that explore the oceans and outer space, robots are all around us. In this nonfiction graphic novel, readers can join Max Axiom and the Society of Super Scientists as they take a closer look at the many kinds of robots and how they make our lives better every day."--Provided by publisher.
Identifiers: LCCN 2022045530 (print) | LCCN 2022045531 (ebook) | ISBN 9781669017370 (hardcover) | ISBN 9781669017325 (paperback) | ISBN 9781669017332 (ebook pdf) | ISBN 9781669017356 (kindle edition) | ISBN 9781669017363 (epub)
Subjects: LCSH: Robots--Juvenile literature. Classification: LCC TJ211.2.C655 2024 (print) | LCC TJ211.2 (ebook) | DDC 670.42/72--dc23/eng/20221206
LC record available at https://lccn.loc.gov/2022045530
LC ebook record available at https://lccn.loc.gov/2022045531

Editorial Credits
Editor: Aaron Sautter; Designer: Elyse White;
Media Researcher: Rebekah Hubstenberger;
Production Specialist: Whitney Schaefer

All internet sites appearing in back matter were available and accurate when this book was sent to press.

TABLE OF CONTENTS

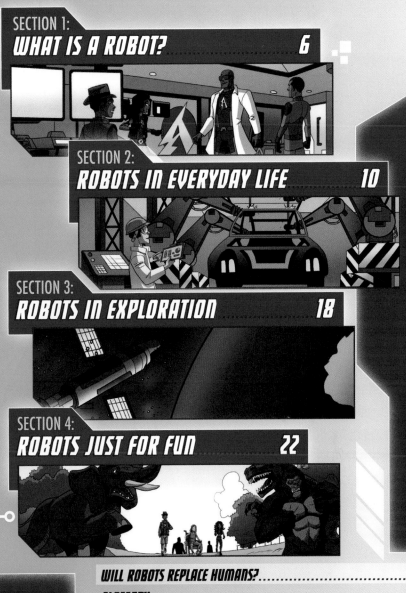

THE SOCIETY OF
SUPER SCIENTISTS

MAX AXIOM

After years of study, Max Axiom, the world's first Super Scientist, knew the mysteries of the universe were too vast for one person alone to uncover. So Max created the Society of Super Scientists! Using their superpowers and super-smarts, this talented group investigates today's most urgent scientific and environmental issues and learns about actions everyone can take to solve them.

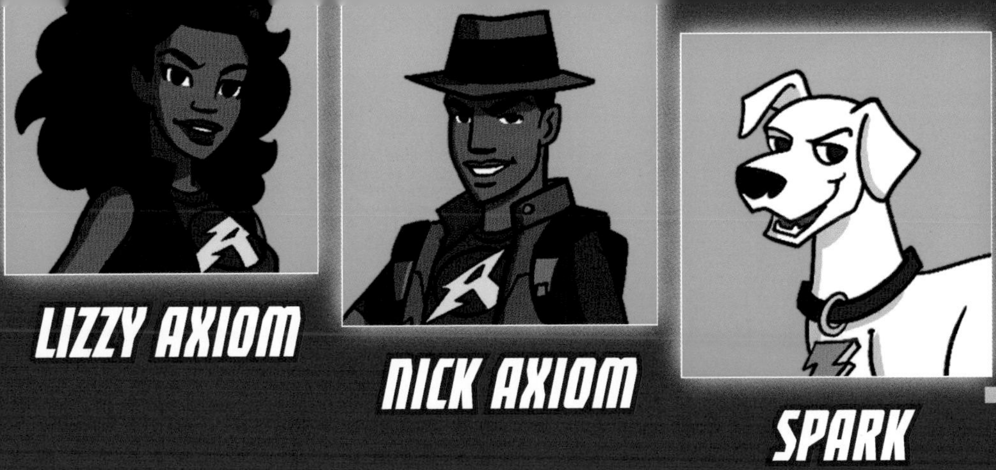
LIZZY AXIOM
NICK AXIOM
SPARK

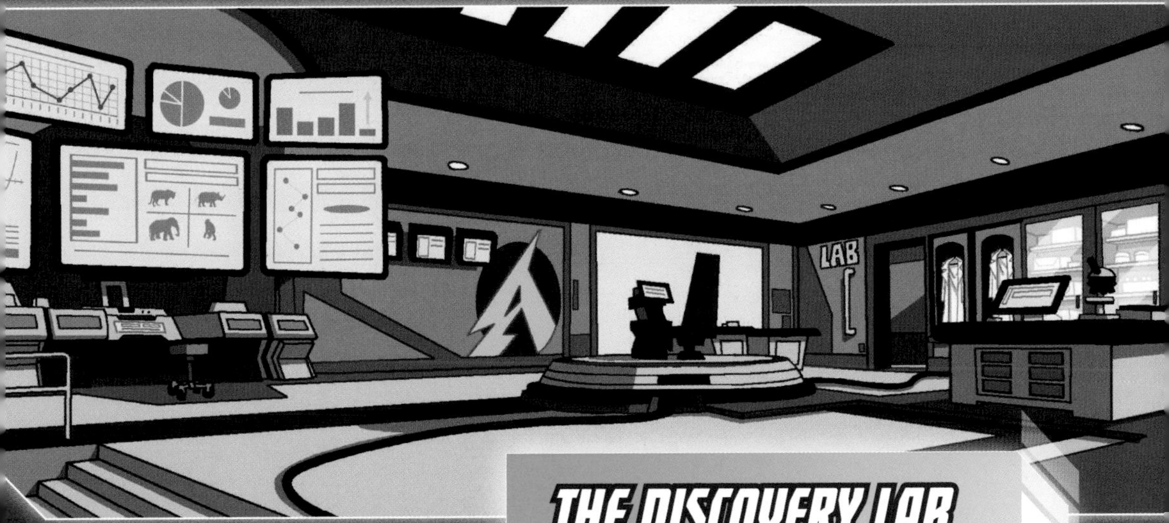

THE DISCOVERY LAB

Home of the Society of Super Scientists, this state-of-the-art lab houses advanced tools for cutting-edge research and radical scientific innovation. More importantly, it is a space for Super Scientists to collaborate and share knowledge as they work together to tackle any challenge.

There are so many different prosthetics! They must help a lot of people.

This is my fifth time here, and it's been so exciting.

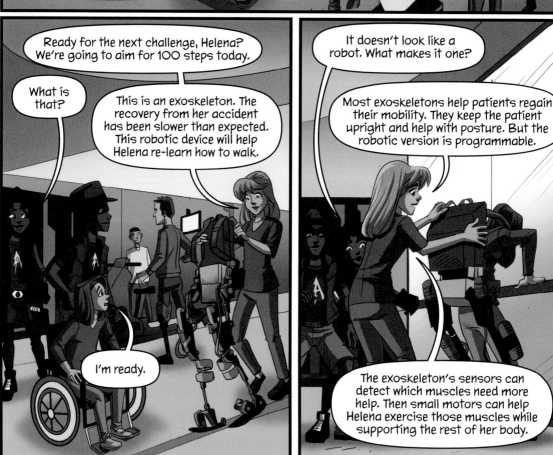

Ready for the next challenge, Helena? We're going to aim for 100 steps today.

What is that?

This is an exoskeleton. The recovery from her accident has been slower than expected. This robotic device will help Helena re-learn how to walk.

I'm ready.

It doesn't look like a robot. What makes it one?

Most exoskeletons help patients regain their mobility. They keep the patient upright and help with posture. But the robotic version is programmable.

The exoskeleton's sensors can detect which muscles need more help. Then small motors can help Helena exercise those muscles while supporting the rest of her body.

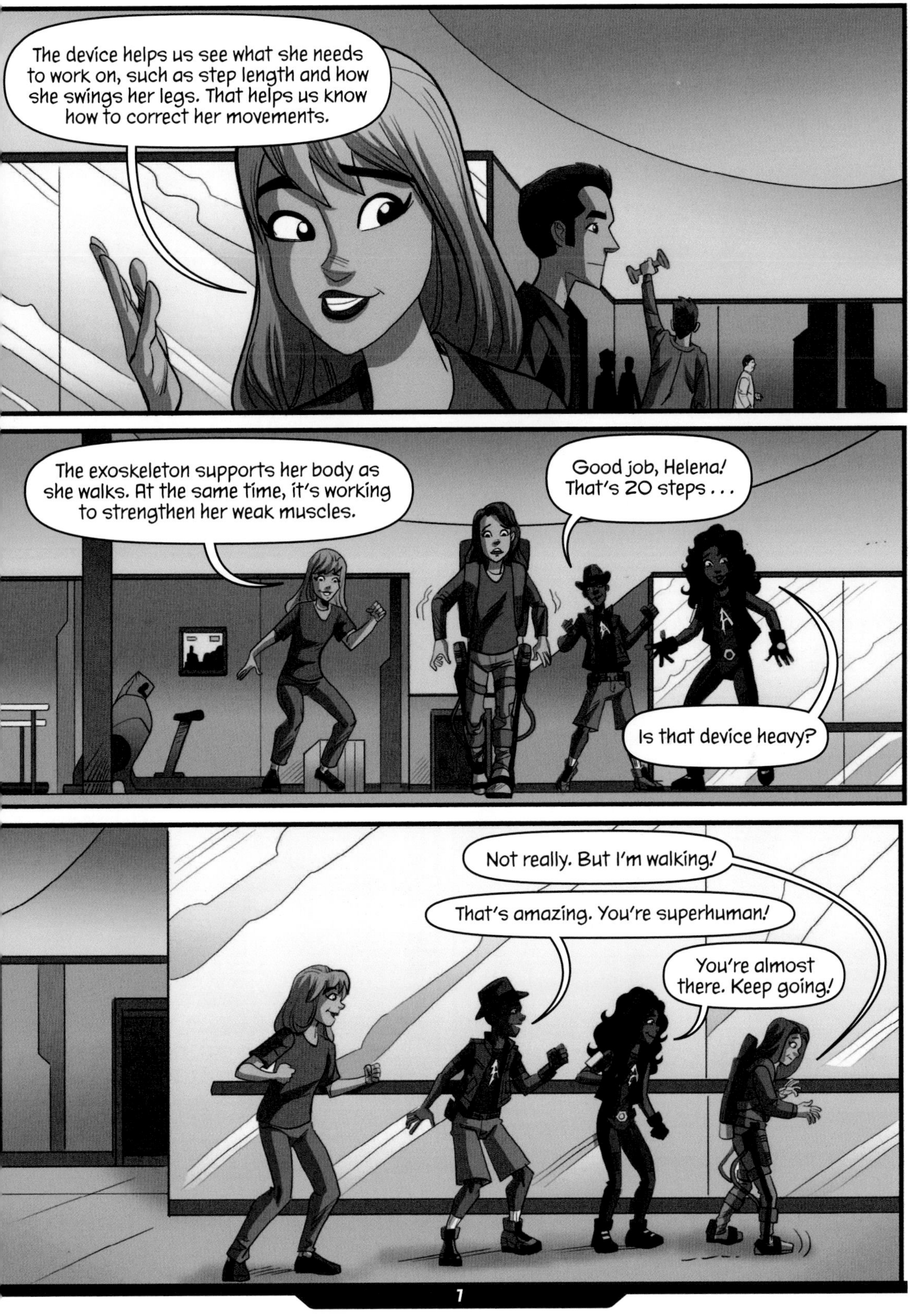
The device helps us see what she needs to work on, such as step length and how she swings her legs. That helps us know how to correct her movements.
The exoskeleton supports her body as she walks. At the same time, it's working to strengthen her weak muscles.
Good job, Helena! That's 20 steps . . .
Is that device heavy?
Not really. But I'm walking!
That's amazing. You're superhuman!
You're almost there. Keep going!

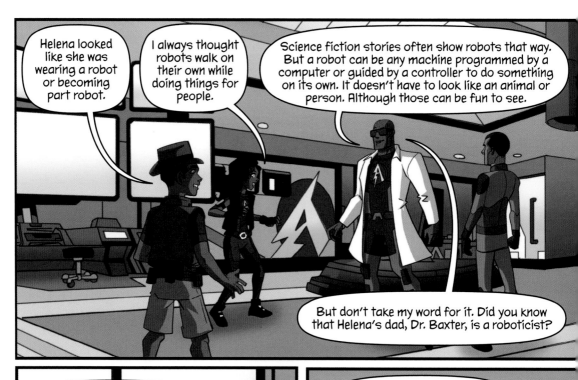

Helena looked like she was wearing a robot or becoming part robot.

I always thought robots walk on their own while doing things for people.

Science fiction stories often show robots that way. But a robot can be any machine programmed by a computer or guided by a controller to do something on its own. It doesn't have to look like an animal or person. Although those can be fun to see.

But don't take my word for it. Did you know that Helena's dad, Dr. Baxter, is a roboticist?

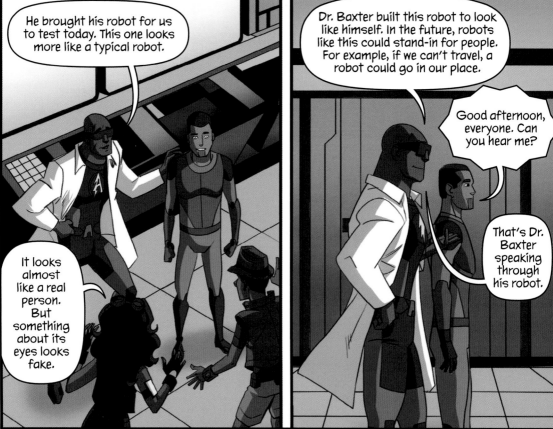

He brought his robot for us to test today. This one looks more like a typical robot.

It looks almost like a real person. But something about its eyes looks fake.

Dr. Baxter built this robot to look like himself. In the future, robots like this could stand-in for people. For example, if we can't travel, a robot could go in our place.

Good afternoon, everyone. Can you hear me?

That's Dr. Baxter speaking through his robot.

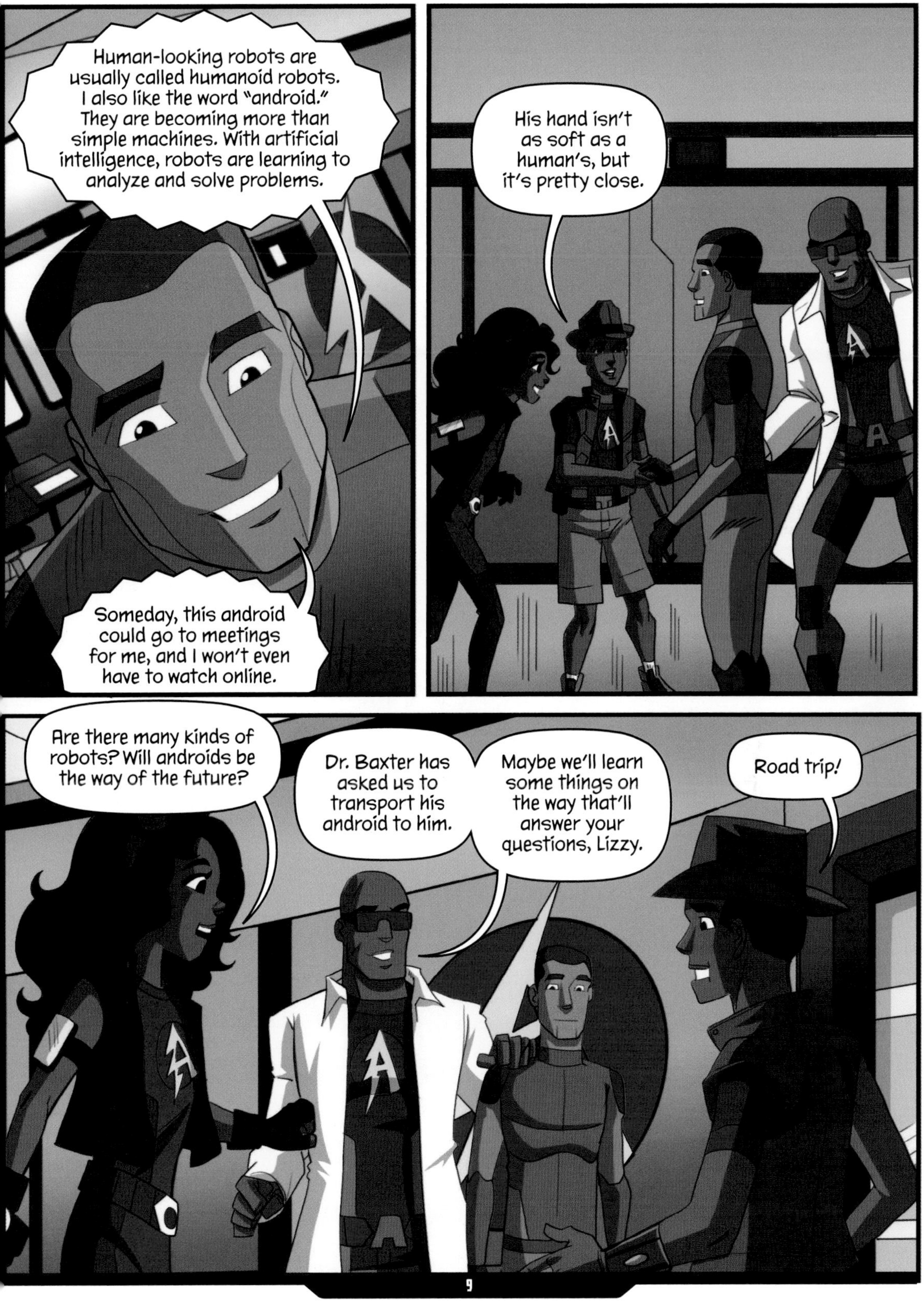
Human-looking robots are usually called humanoid robots. I also like the word "android." They are becoming more than simple machines. With artificial intelligence, robots are learning to analyze and solve problems.
Someday, this android could go to meetings for me, and I won't even have to watch online.
His hand isn't as soft as a human's, but it's pretty close.
Are there many kinds of robots? Will androids be the way of the future?
Dr. Baxter has asked us to transport his android to him.
Maybe we'll learn some things on the way that'll answer your questions, Lizzy.
Road trip!

SECTION 2: *ROBOTS IN EVERYDAY LIFE*

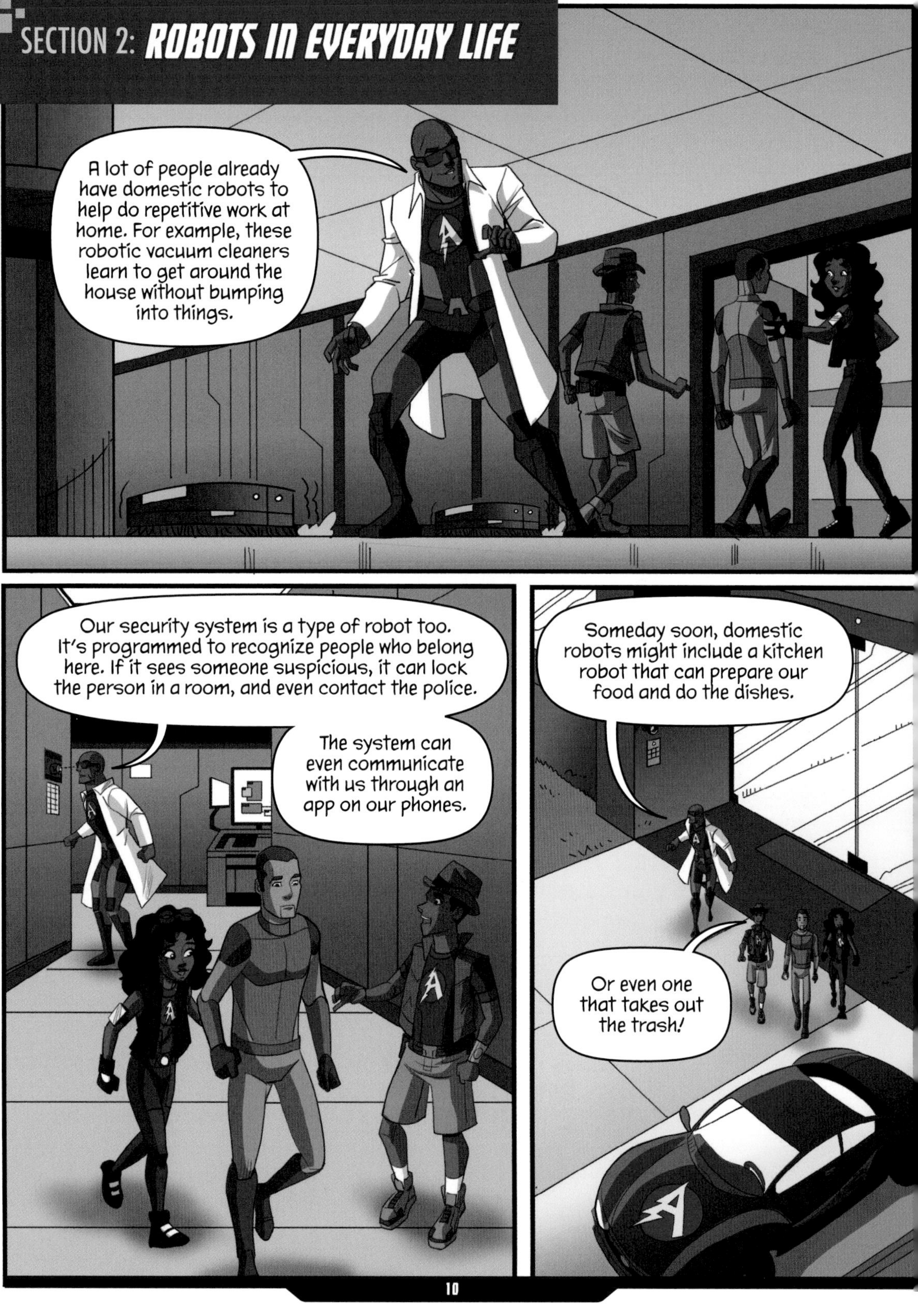
A lot of people already have domestic robots to help do repetitive work at home. For example, these robotic vacuum cleaners learn to get around the house without bumping into things.
Our security system is a type of robot too. It's programmed to recognize people who belong here. If it sees someone suspicious, it can lock the person in a room, and even contact the police.
The system can even communicate with us through an app on our phones.
Someday soon, domestic robots might include a kitchen robot that can prepare our food and do the dishes.
Or even one that takes out the trash!

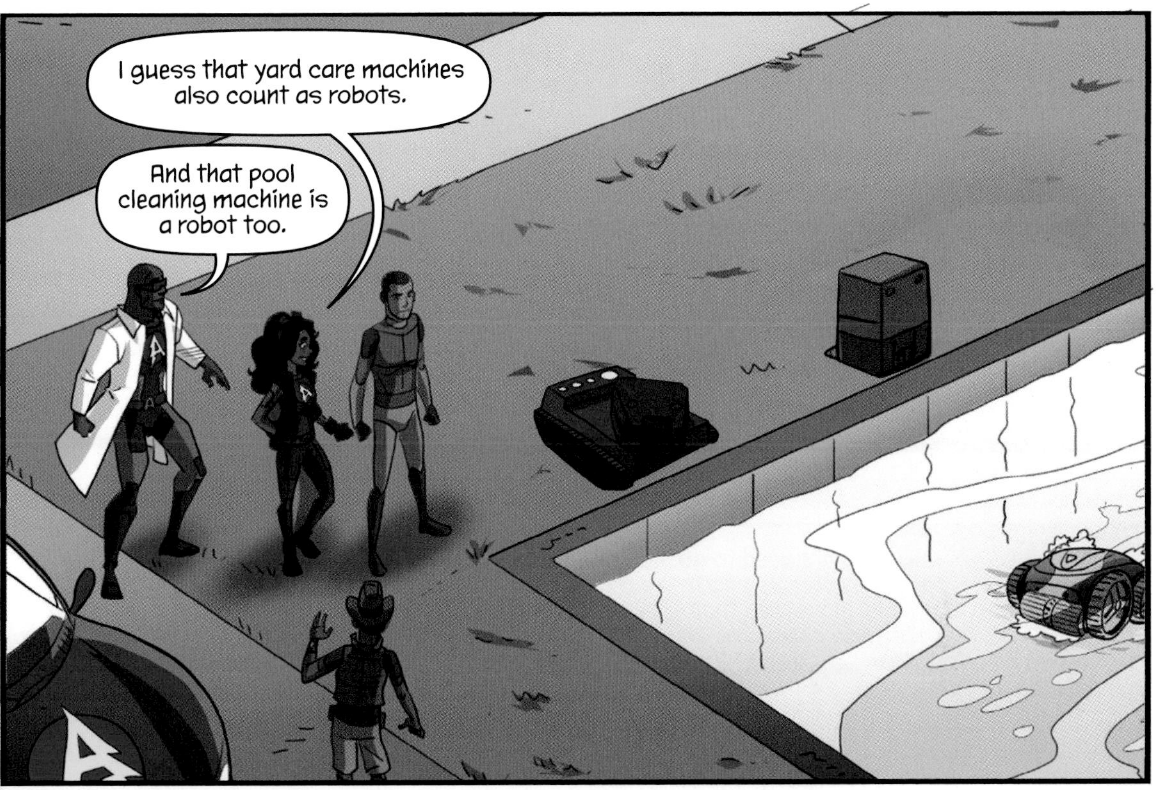
I guess that yard care machines also count as robots.
And that pool cleaning machine is a robot too.

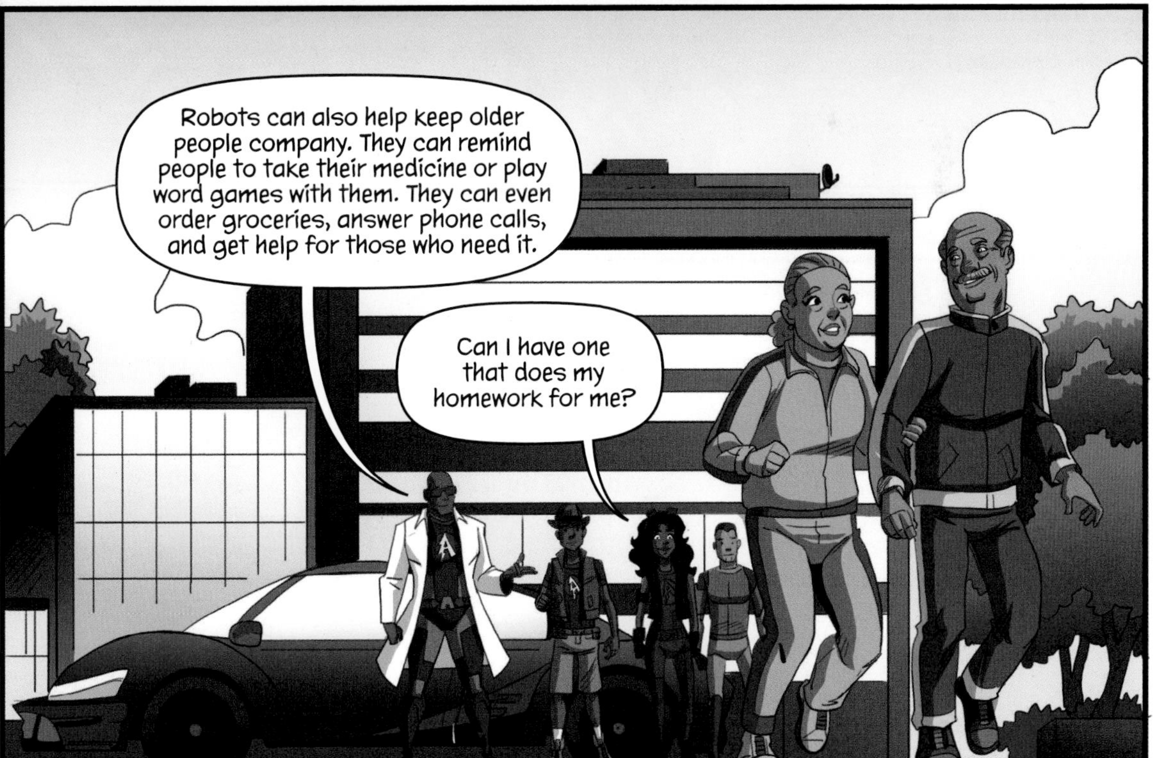
Robots can also help keep older people company. They can remind people to take their medicine or play word games with them. They can even order groceries, answer phone calls, and get help for those who need it.
Can I have one that does my homework for me?

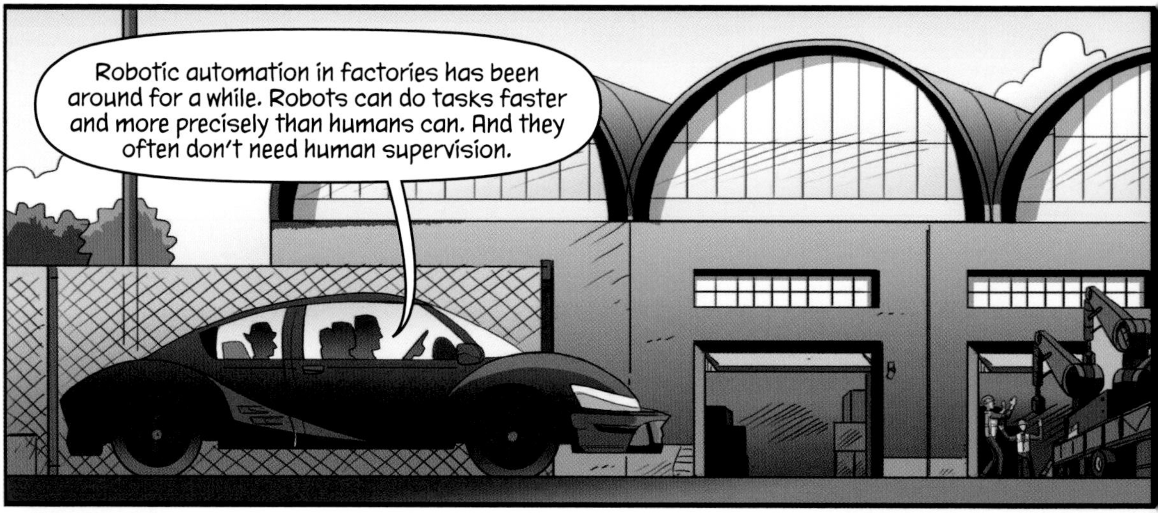
Robotic automation in factories has been around for a while. Robots can do tasks faster and more precisely than humans can. And they often don't need human supervision.

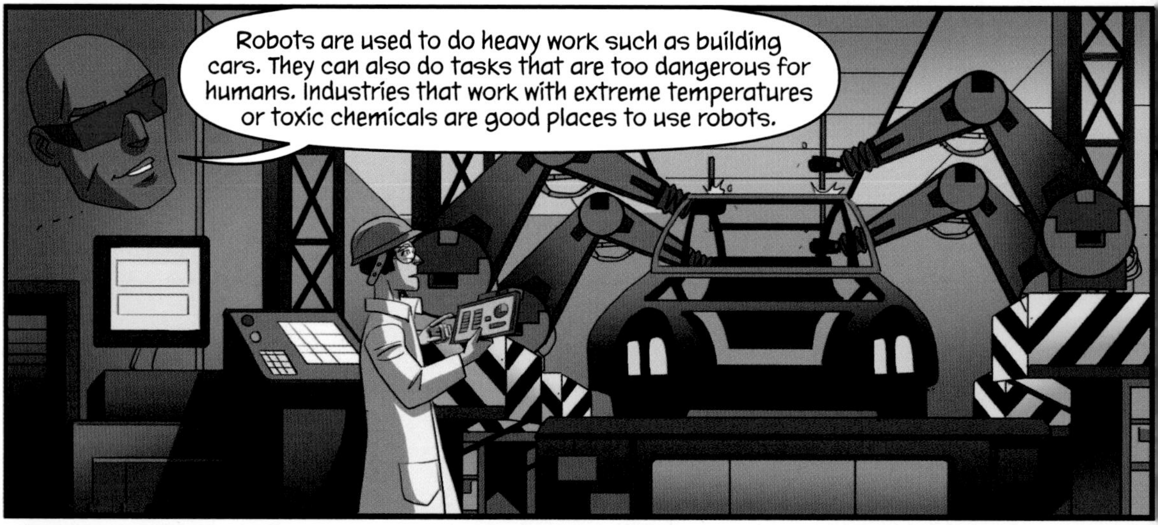
Robots are used to do heavy work such as building cars. They can also do tasks that are too dangerous for humans. Industries that work with extreme temperatures or toxic chemicals are good places to use robots.

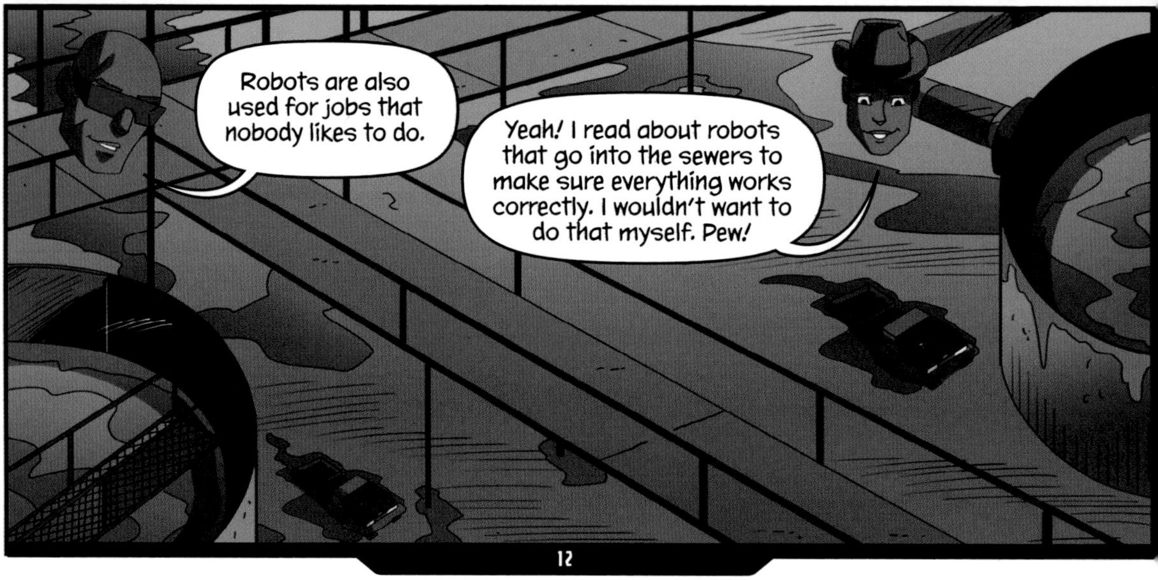
Robots are also used for jobs that nobody likes to do.
Yeah! I read about robots that go into the sewers to make sure everything works correctly. I wouldn't want to do that myself. Pew!

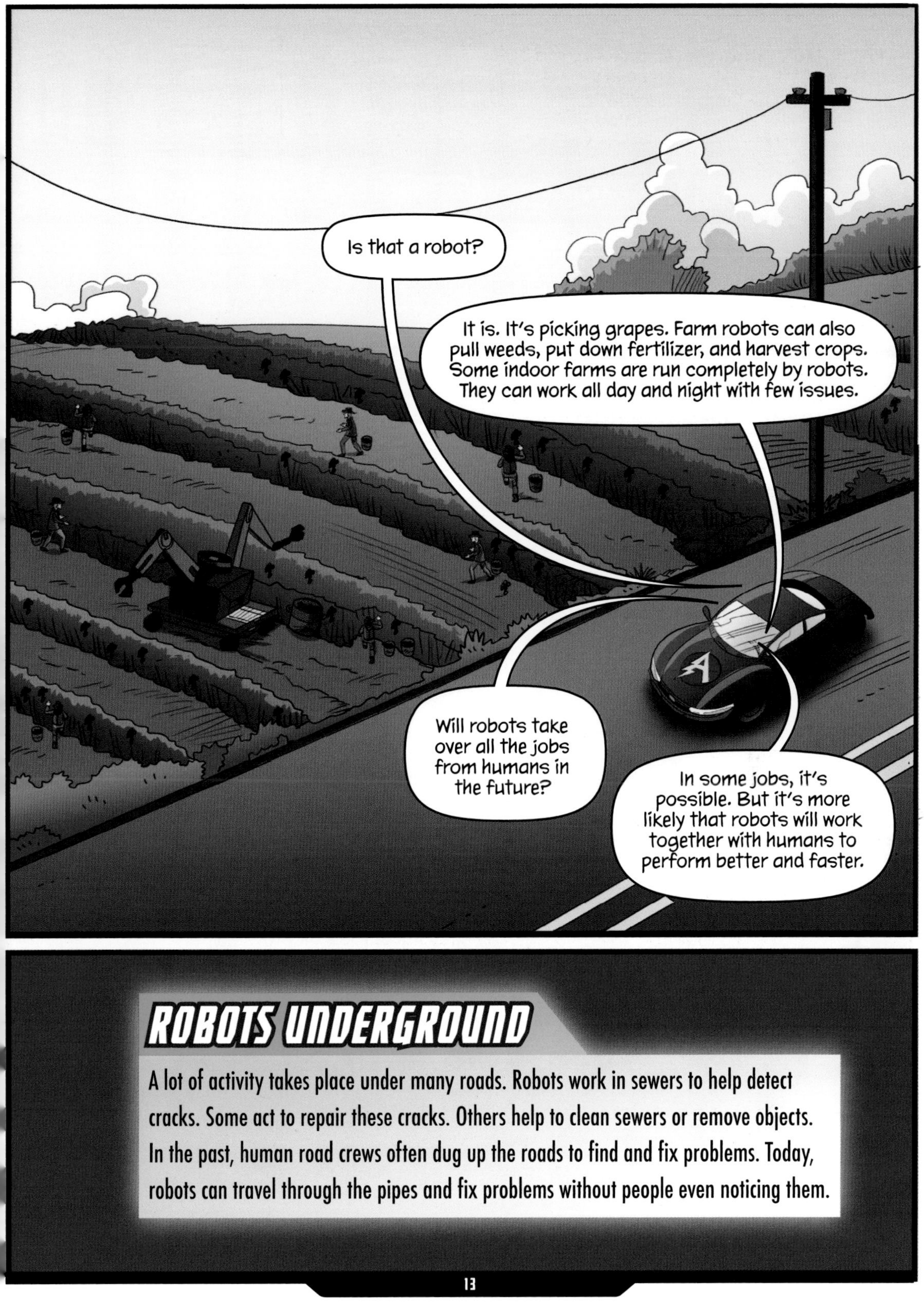
Is that a robot?
It is. It's picking grapes. Farm robots can also pull weeds, put down fertilizer, and harvest crops. Some indoor farms are run completely by robots. They can work all day and night with few issues.
Will robots take over all the jobs from humans in the future?
In some jobs, it's possible. But it's more likely that robots will work together with humans to perform better and faster.

ROBOTS UNDERGROUND

A lot of activity takes place under many roads. Robots work in sewers to help detect cracks. Some act to repair these cracks. Others help to clean sewers or remove objects. In the past, human road crews often dug up the roads to find and fix problems. Today, robots can travel through the pipes and fix problems without people even noticing them.

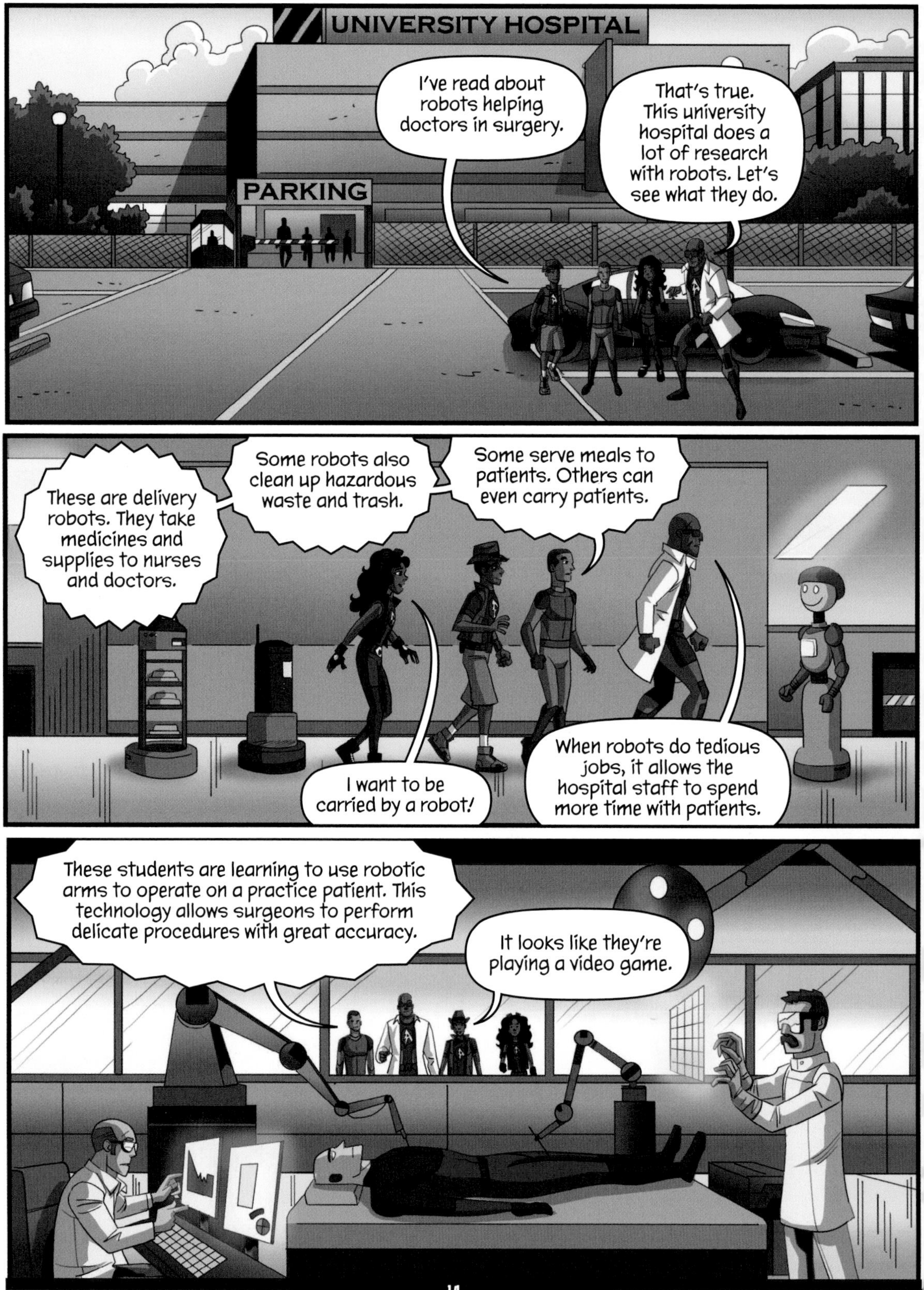
UNIVERSITY HOSPITAL
PARKING
I've read about robots helping doctors in surgery.
That's true. This university hospital does a lot of research with robots. Let's see what they do.
These are delivery robots. They take medicines and supplies to nurses and doctors.
Some robots also clean up hazardous waste and trash.
Some serve meals to patients. Others can even carry patients.
I want to be carried by a robot!
When robots do tedious jobs, it allows the hospital staff to spend more time with patients.
These students are learning to use robotic arms to operate on a practice patient. This technology allows surgeons to perform delicate procedures with great accuracy.
It looks like they're playing a video game.

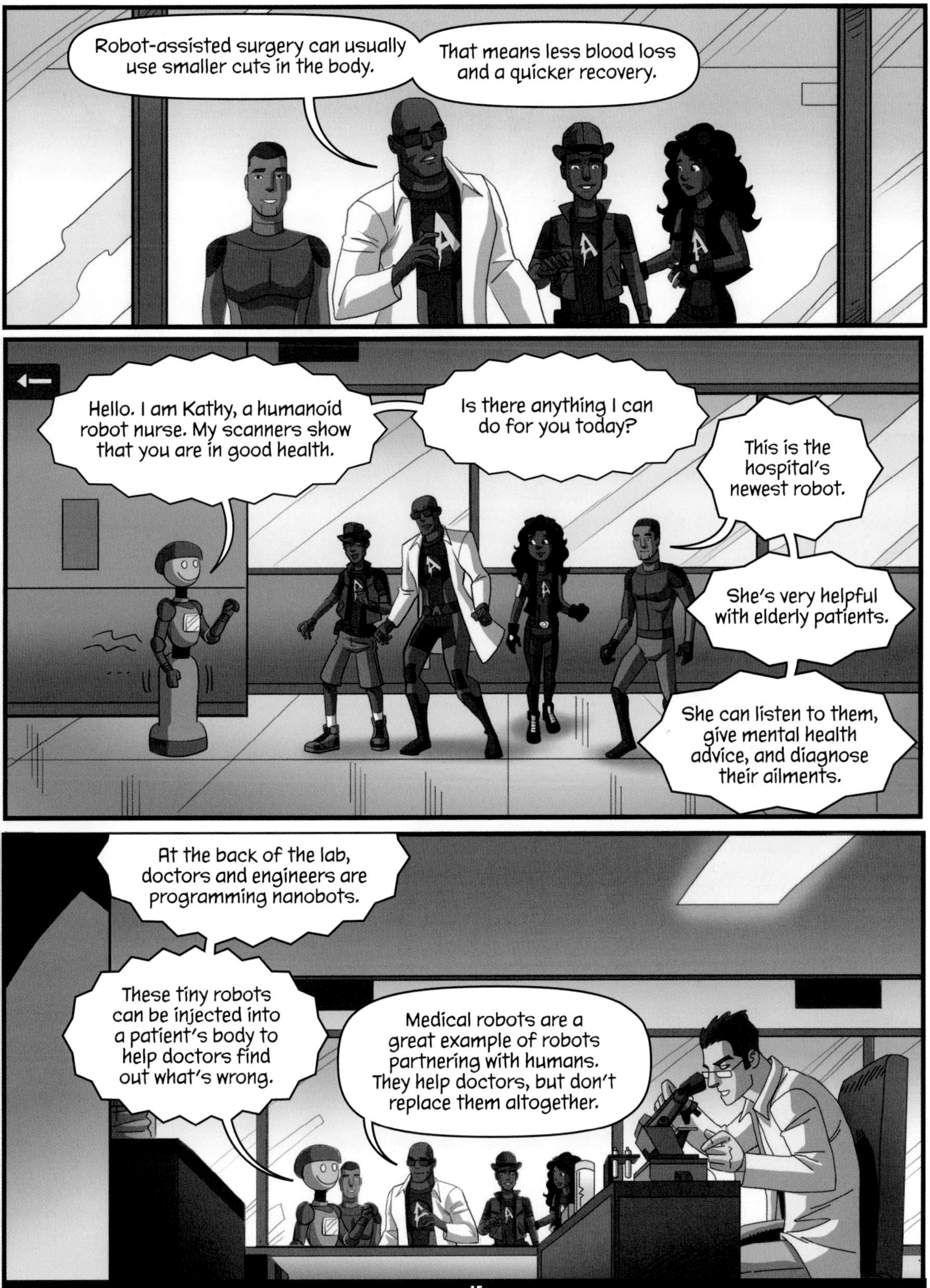
Robot-assisted surgery can usually use smaller cuts in the body.
That means less blood loss and a quicker recovery.
Hello. I am Kathy, a humanoid robot nurse. My scanners show that you are in good health.
Is there anything I can do for you today?
This is the hospital's newest robot.
She's very helpful with elderly patients.
She can listen to them, give mental health advice, and diagnose their ailments.
At the back of the lab, doctors and engineers are programming nanobots.
These tiny robots can be injected into a patient's body to help doctors find out what's wrong.
Medical robots are a great example of robots partnering with humans. They help doctors, but don't replace them altogether.

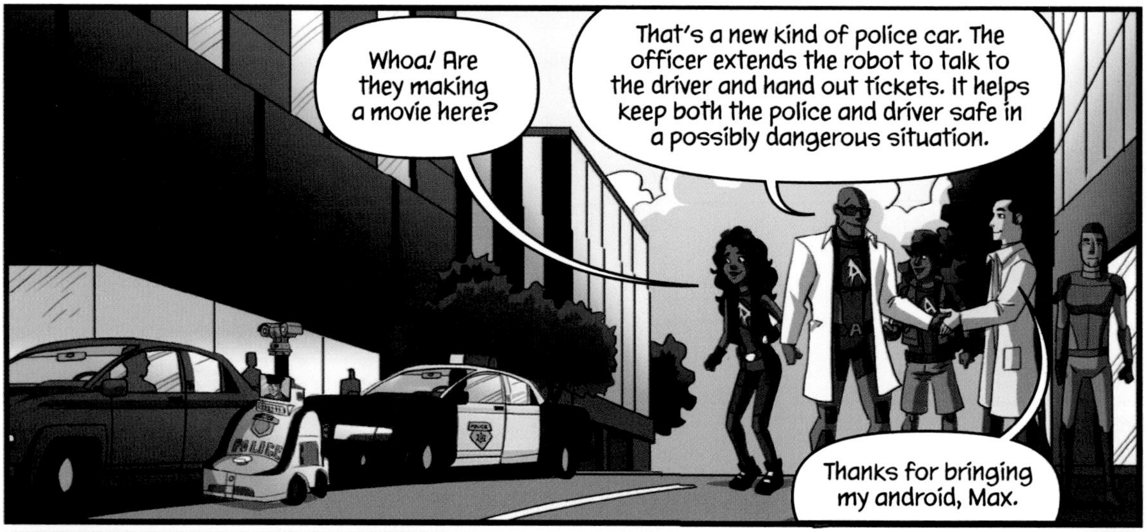
Whoa! Are they making a movie here?
That's a new kind of police car. The officer extends the robot to talk to the driver and hand out tickets. It helps keep both the police and driver safe in a possibly dangerous situation.
Thanks for bringing my android, Max.

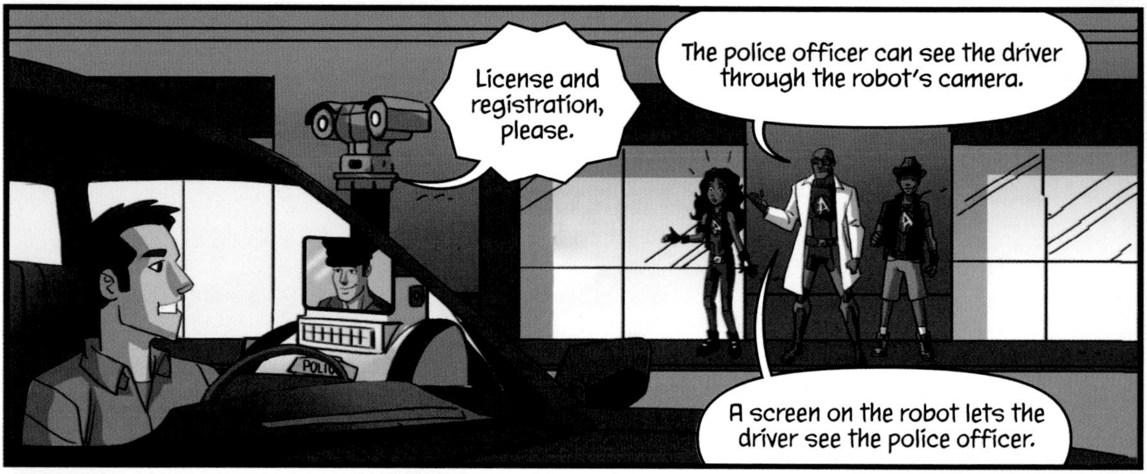
License and registration, please.
The police officer can see the driver through the robot's camera.
A screen on the robot lets the driver see the police officer.

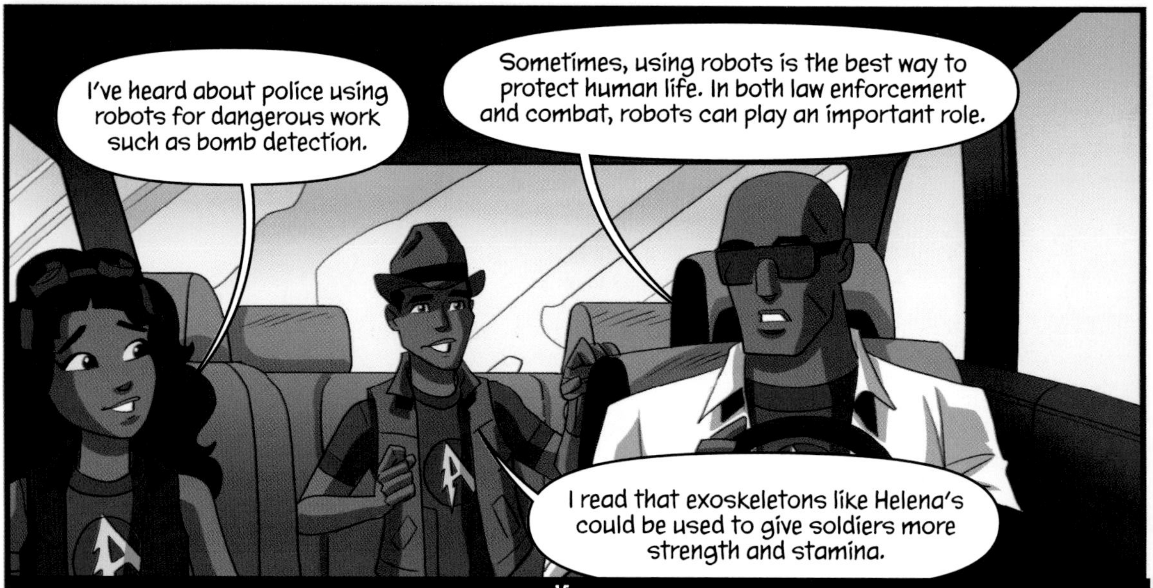
I've heard about police using robots for dangerous work such as bomb detection.
Sometimes, using robots is the best way to protect human life. In both law enforcement and combat, robots can play an important role.
I read that exoskeletons like Helena's could be used to give soldiers more strength and stamina.

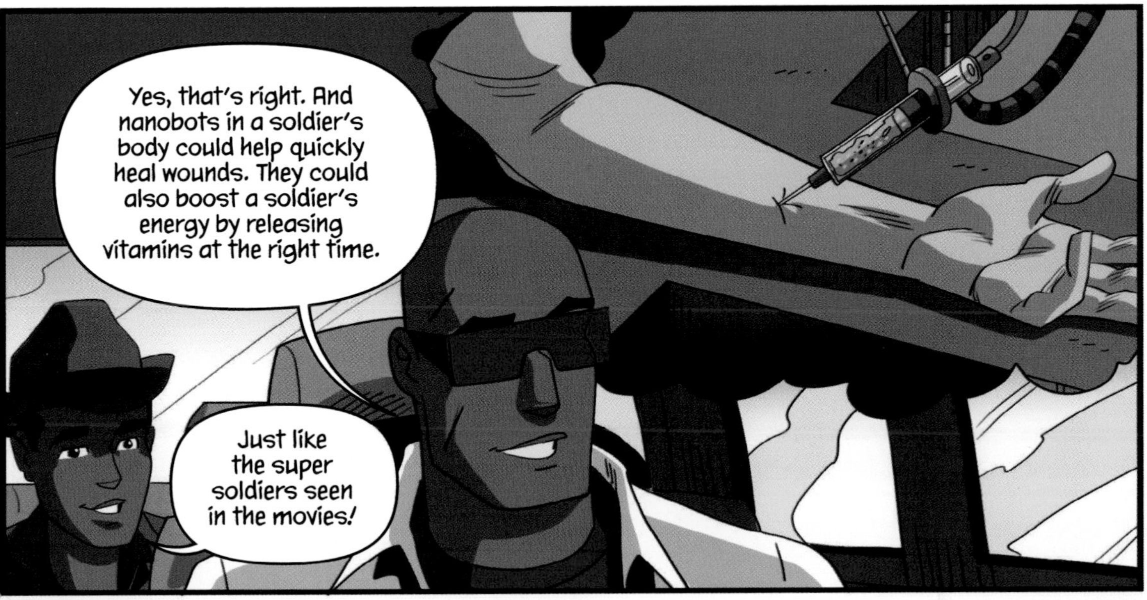
Yes, that's right. And nanobots in a soldier's body could help quickly heal wounds. They could also boost a soldier's energy by releasing vitamins at the right time.
Just like the super soldiers seen in the movies!

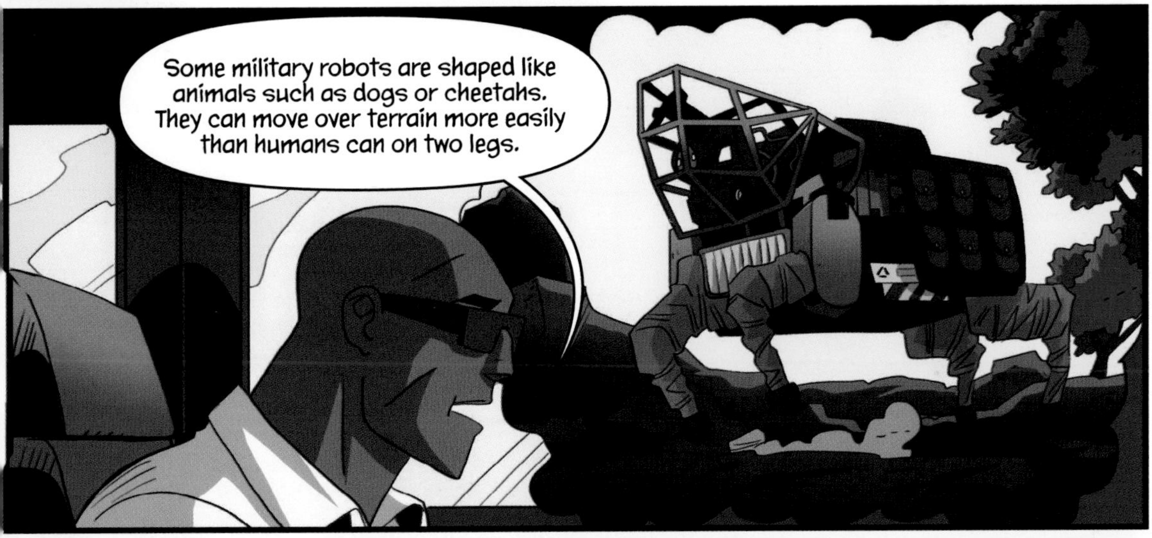
Some military robots are shaped like animals such as dogs or cheetahs. They can move over terrain more easily than humans can on two legs.

DOG-SHAPED SOLDIER

AlphaDog, built by Boston Dynamics, is a four-legged robot that's the size of a donkey. It can carry heavy items over difficult terrain or bring supplies to soldiers in the field. It can carry loads of up to 400 pounds (181 kilograms.)

SECTION 3: ROBOTS IN EXPLORATION

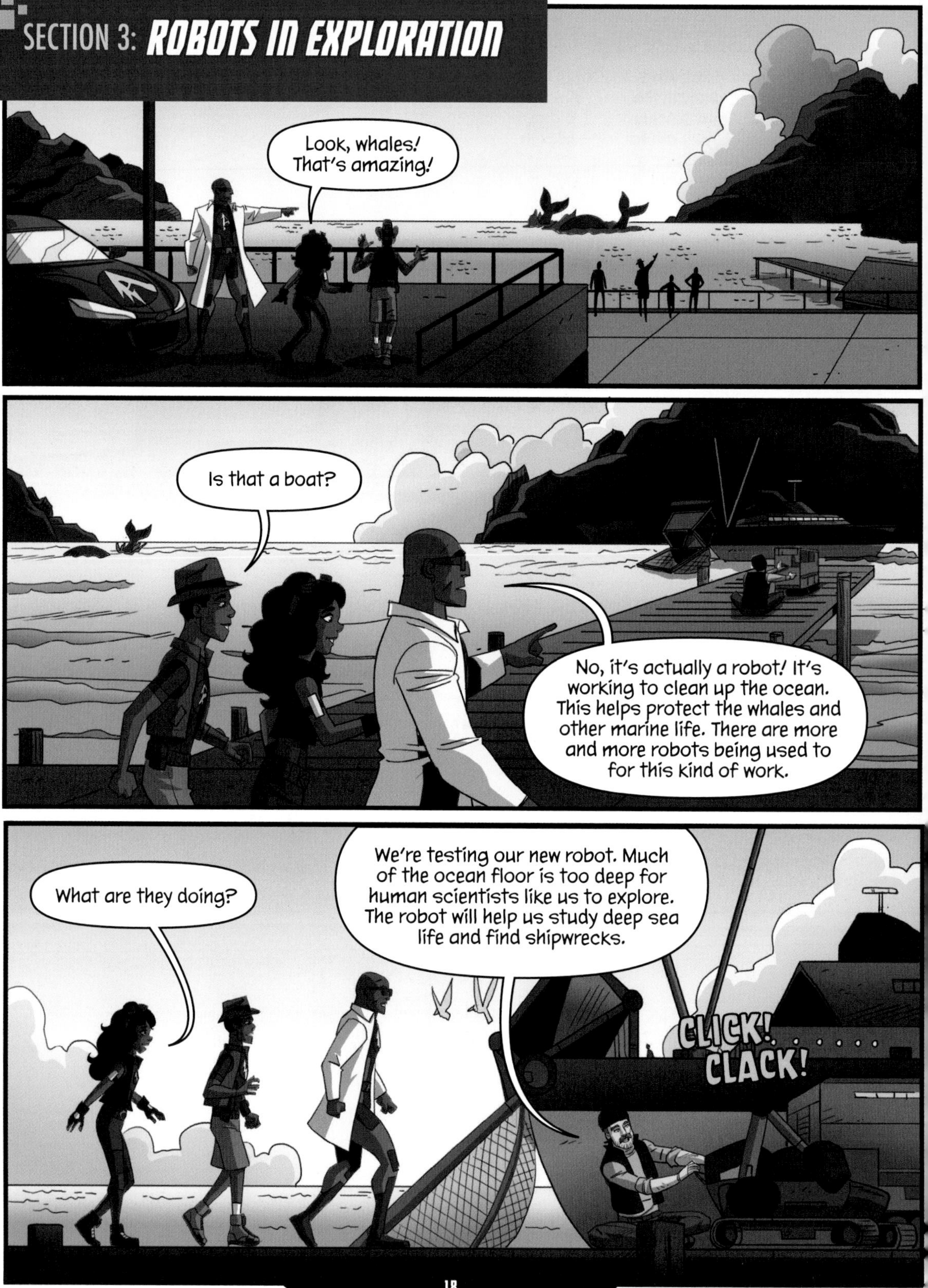

Look, whales! That's amazing!
Is that a boat?
No, it's actually a robot! It's working to clean up the ocean. This helps protect the whales and other marine life. There are more and more robots being used to for this kind of work.
What are they doing?
We're testing our new robot. Much of the ocean floor is too deep for human scientists like us to explore. The robot will help us study deep sea life and find shipwrecks.
CLICK! CLACK!

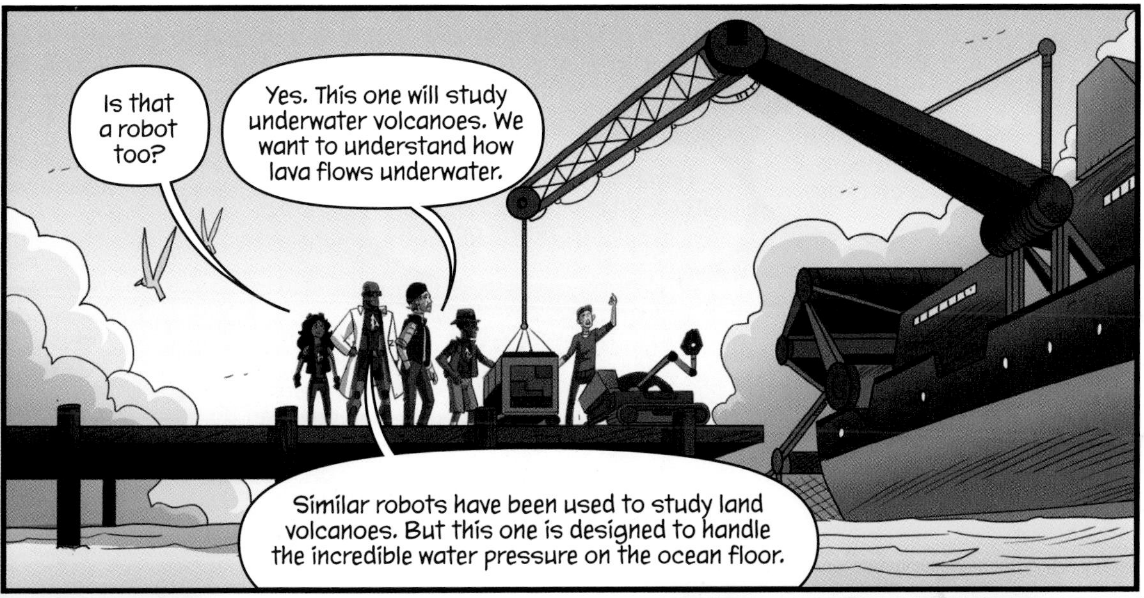
Is that a robot too?
Yes. This one will study underwater volcanoes. We want to understand how lava flows underwater.
Similar robots have been used to study land volcanoes. But this one is designed to handle the incredible water pressure on the ocean floor.

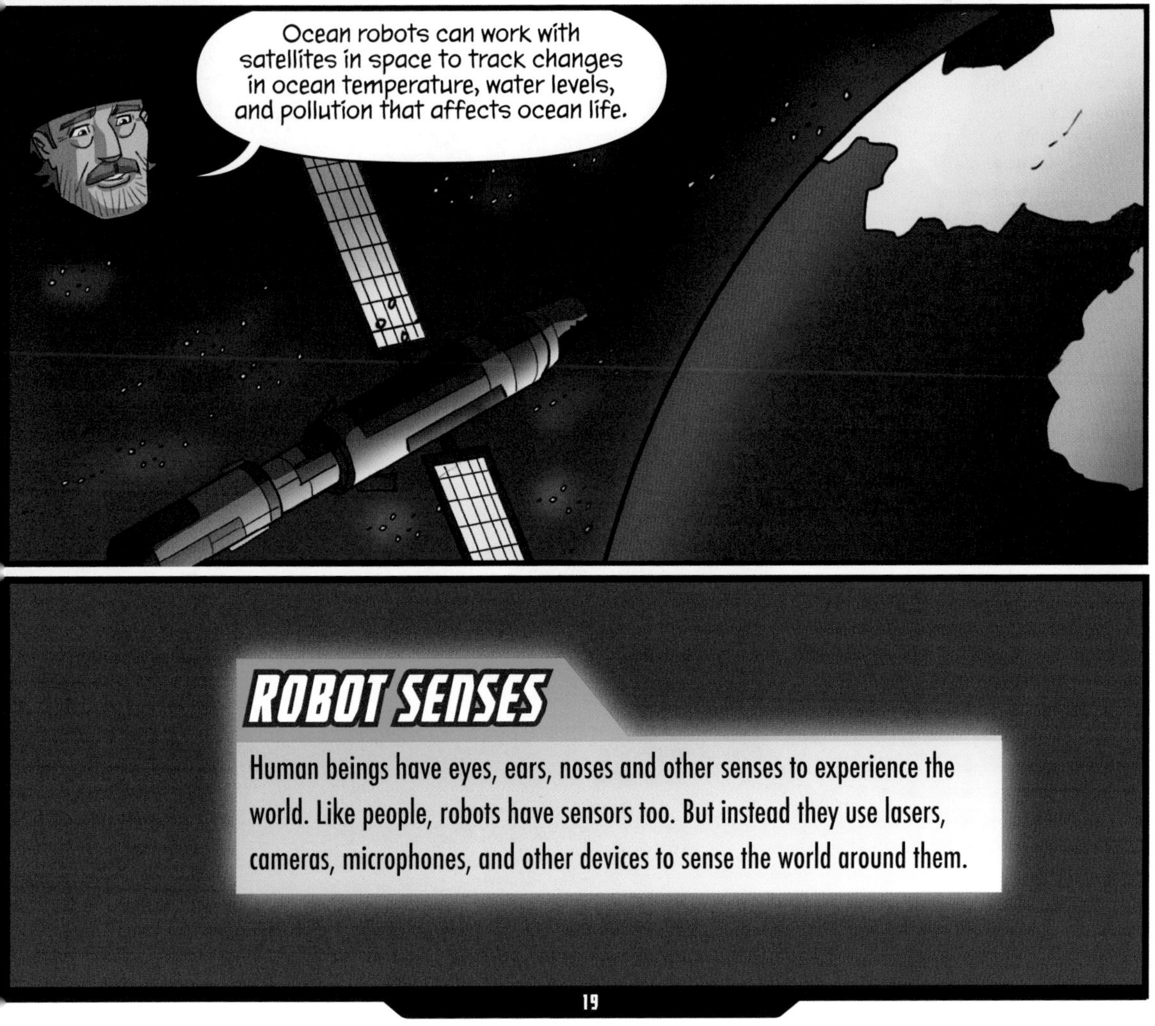
Ocean robots can work with satellites in space to track changes in ocean temperature, water levels, and pollution that affects ocean life.

ROBOT SENSES

Human beings have eyes, ears, noses and other senses to experience the world. Like people, robots have sensors too. But instead they use lasers, cameras, microphones, and other devices to sense the world around them.

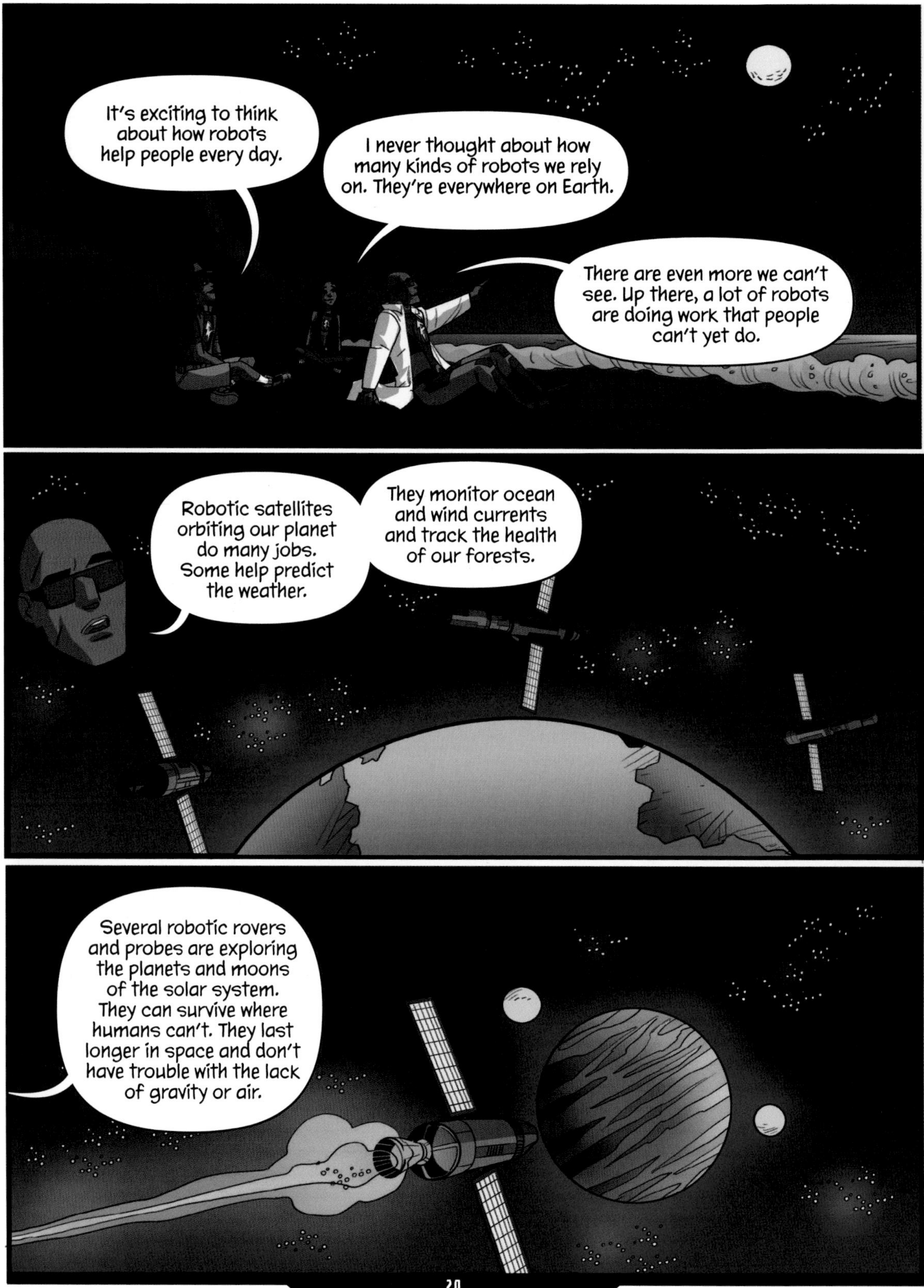
It's exciting to think about how robots help people every day.
I never thought about how many kinds of robots we rely on. They're everywhere on Earth.
There are even more we can't see. Up there, a lot of robots are doing work that people can't yet do.
Robotic satellites orbiting our planet do many jobs. Some help predict the weather.
They monitor ocean and wind currents and track the health of our forests.
Several robotic rovers and probes are exploring the planets and moons of the solar system. They can survive where humans can't. They last longer in space and don't have trouble with the lack of gravity or air.

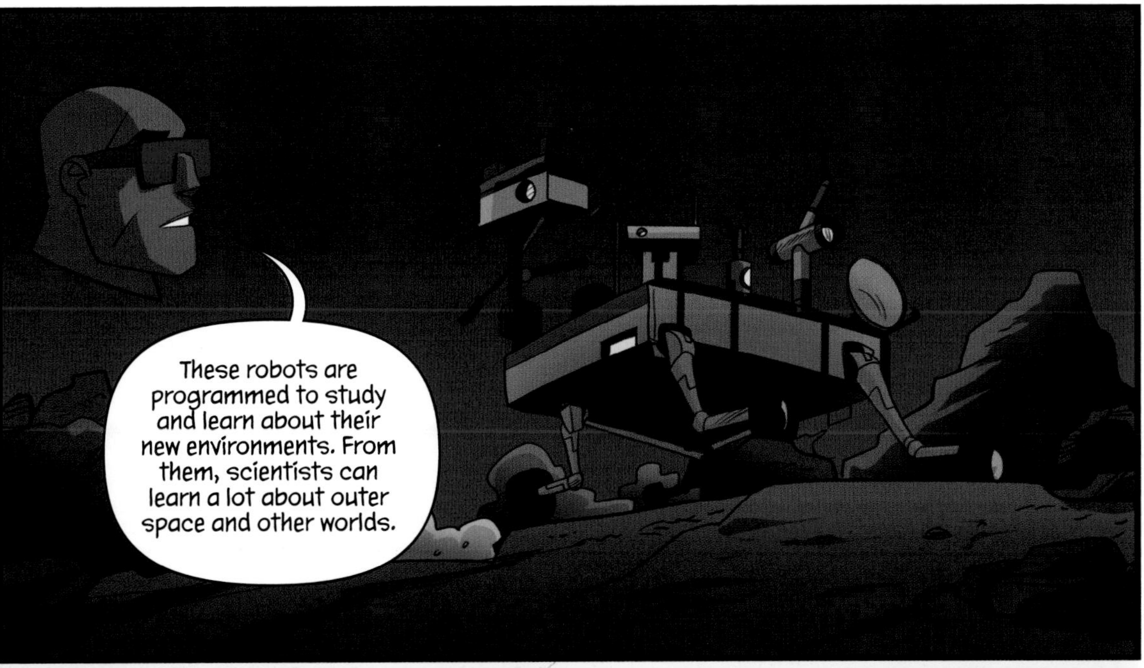
These robots are programmed to study and learn about their new environments. From them, scientists can learn a lot about outer space and other worlds.

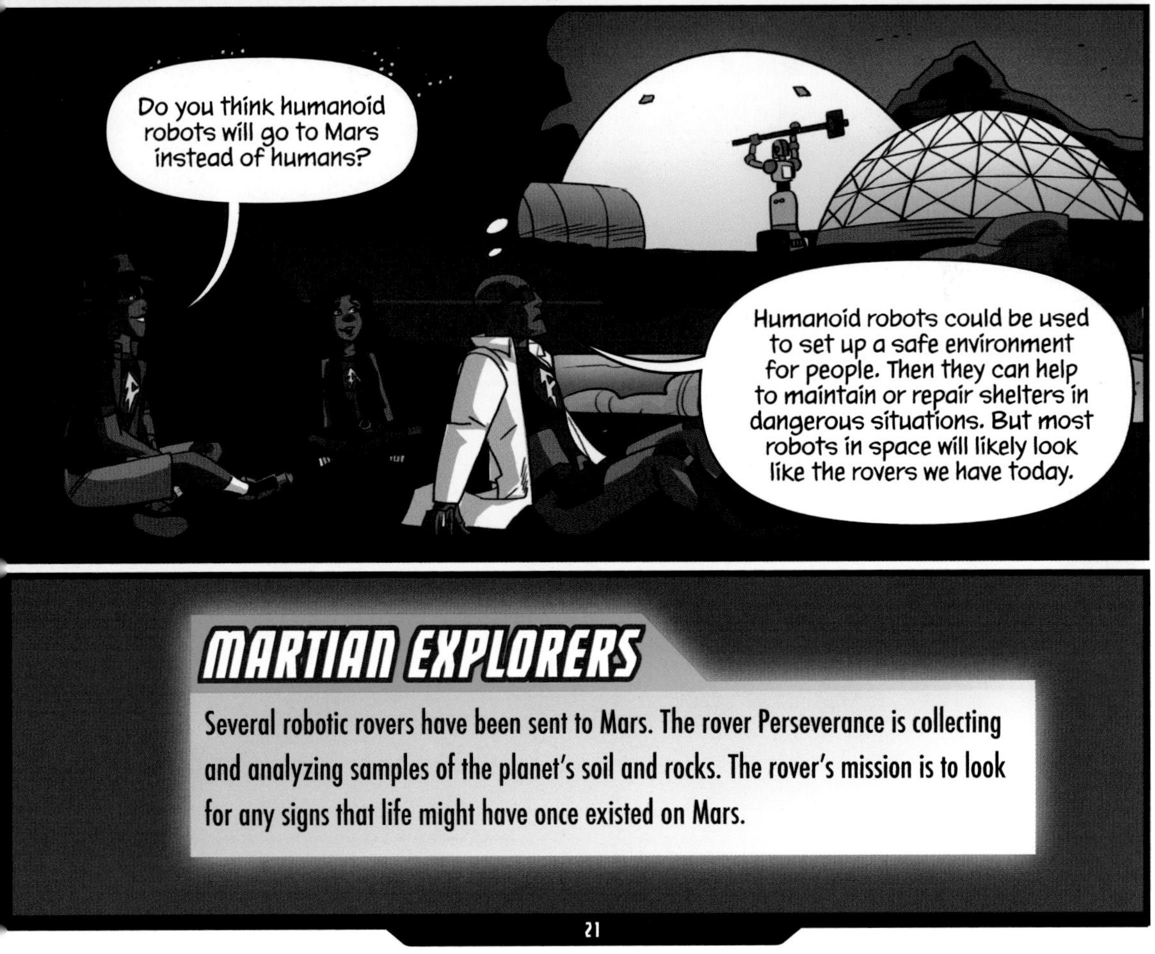
Do you think humanoid robots will go to Mars instead of humans?
Humanoid robots could be used to set up a safe environment for people. Then they can help to maintain or repair shelters in dangerous situations. But most robots in space will likely look like the rovers we have today.

MARTIAN EXPLORERS

Several robotic rovers have been sent to Mars. The rover Perseverance is collecting and analyzing samples of the planet's soil and rocks. The rover's mission is to look for any signs that life might have once existed on Mars.

SECTION 4: ROBOTS JUST FOR FUN

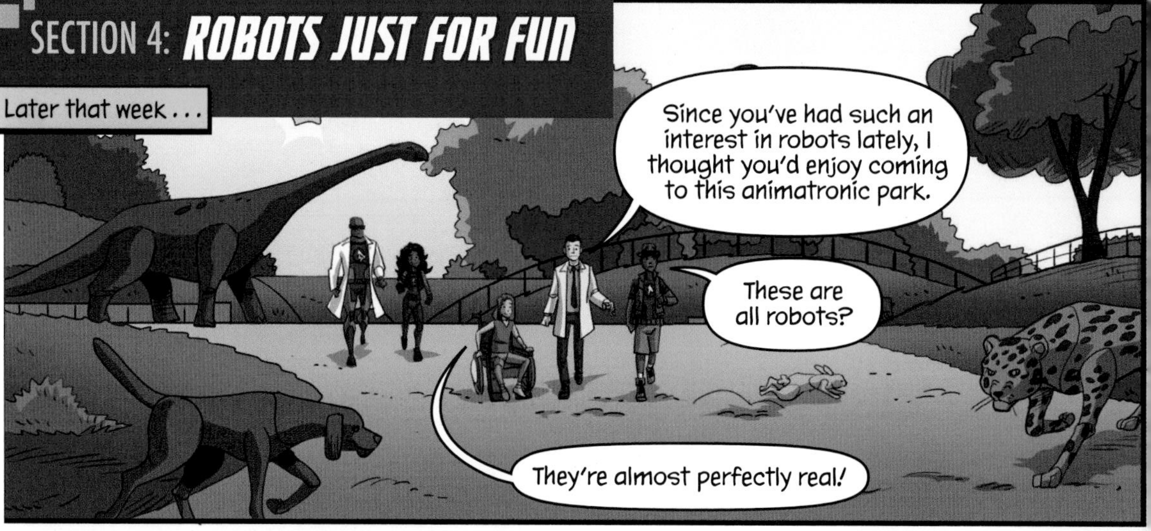

Later that week . . .
Since you've had such an interest in robots lately, I thought you'd enjoy coming to this animatronic park.
These are all robots?
They're almost perfectly real!

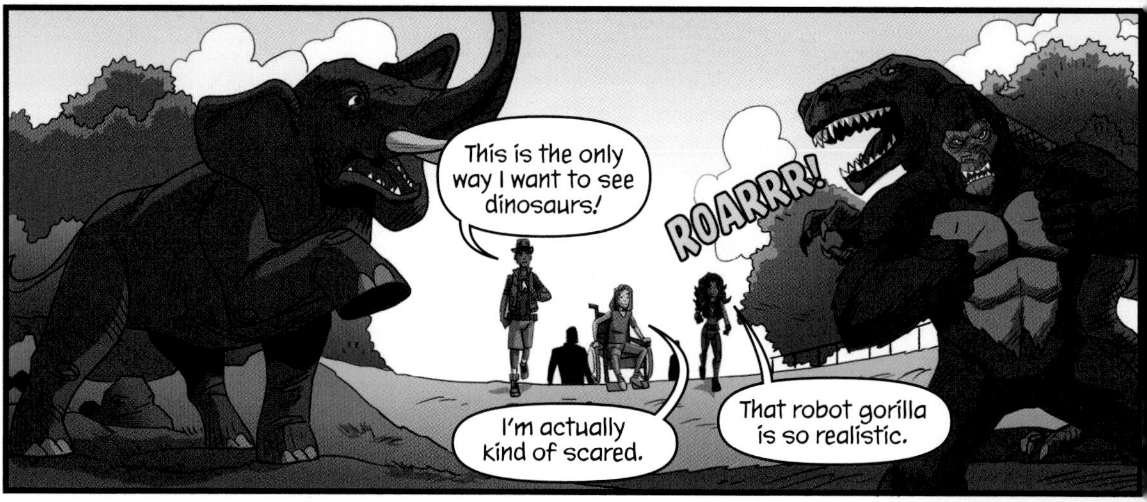

This is the only way I want to see dinosaurs!
ROARRR!
I'm actually kind of scared.
That robot gorilla is so realistic.

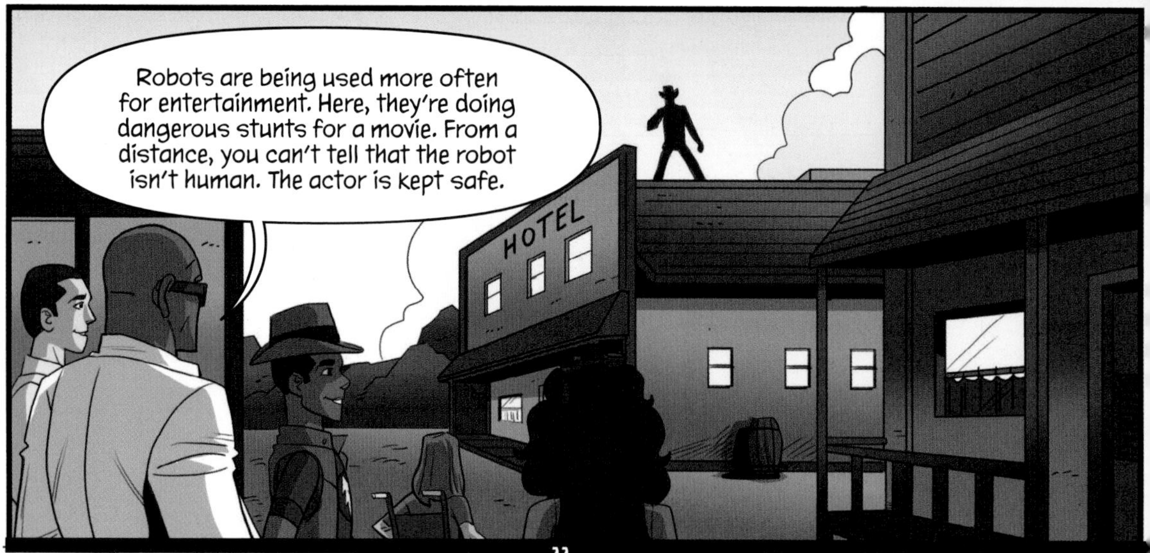

Robots are being used more often for entertainment. Here, they're doing dangerous stunts for a movie. From a distance, you can't tell that the robot isn't human. The actor is kept safe.
HOTEL

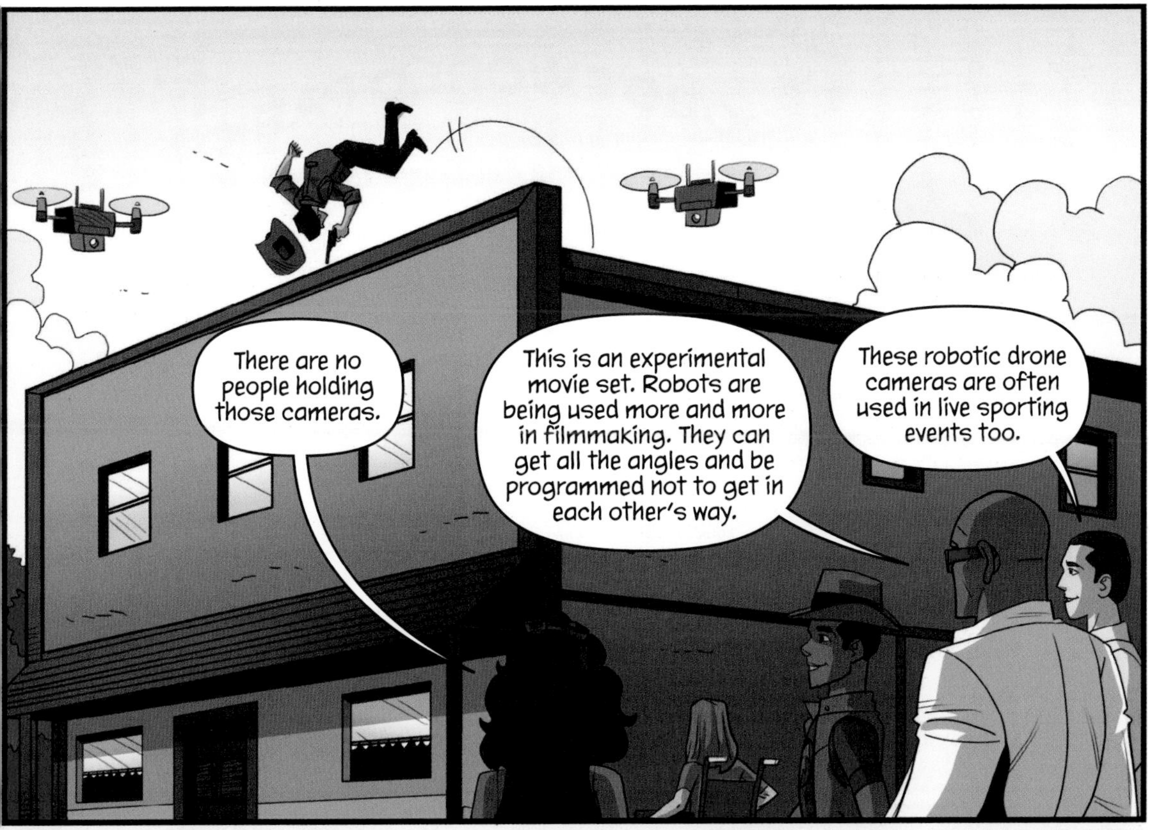
There are no people holding those cameras.
This is an experimental movie set. Robots are being used more and more in filmmaking. They can get all the angles and be programmed not to get in each other's way.
These robotic drone cameras are often used in live sporting events too.

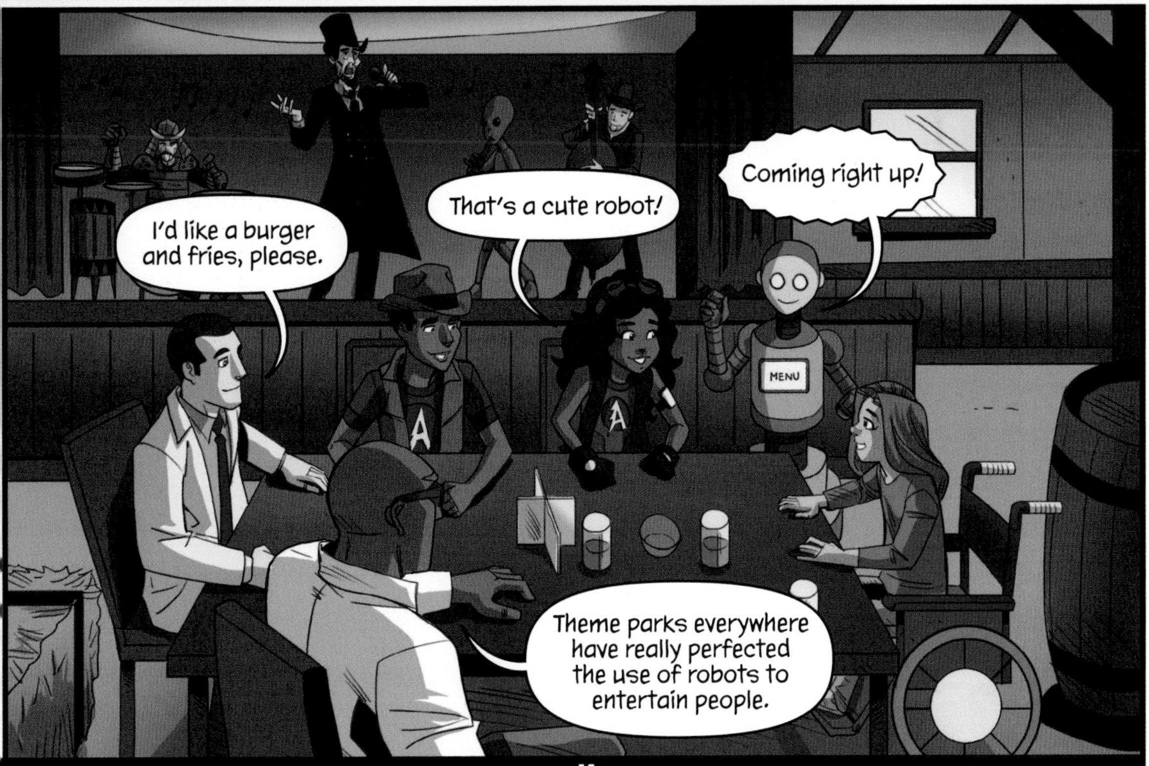
I'd like a burger and fries, please.
That's a cute robot!
Coming right up!
MENU
Theme parks everywhere have really perfected the use of robots to entertain people.

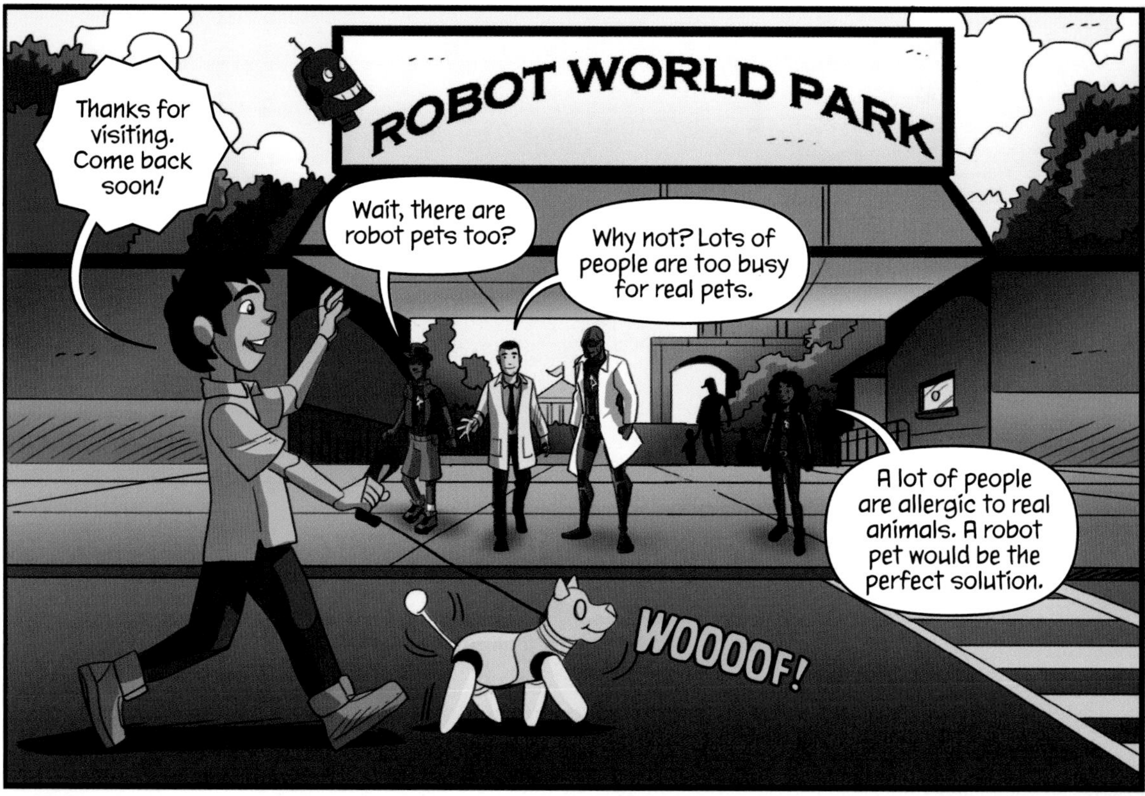
ROBOT WORLD PARK
Thanks for visiting. Come back soon!
Wait, there are robot pets too?
Why not? Lots of people are too busy for real pets.
A lot of people are allergic to real animals. A robot pet would be the perfect solution.
WOOOOF!

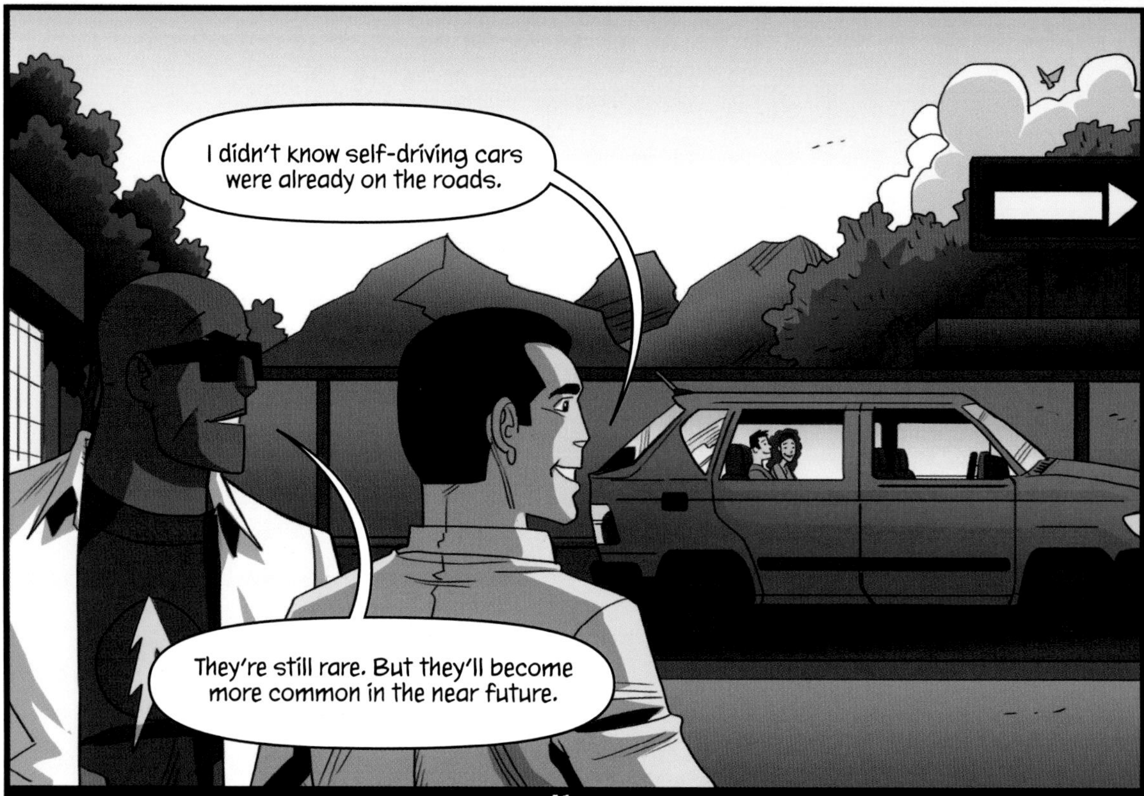
I didn't know self-driving cars were already on the roads.
They're still rare. But they'll become more common in the near future.

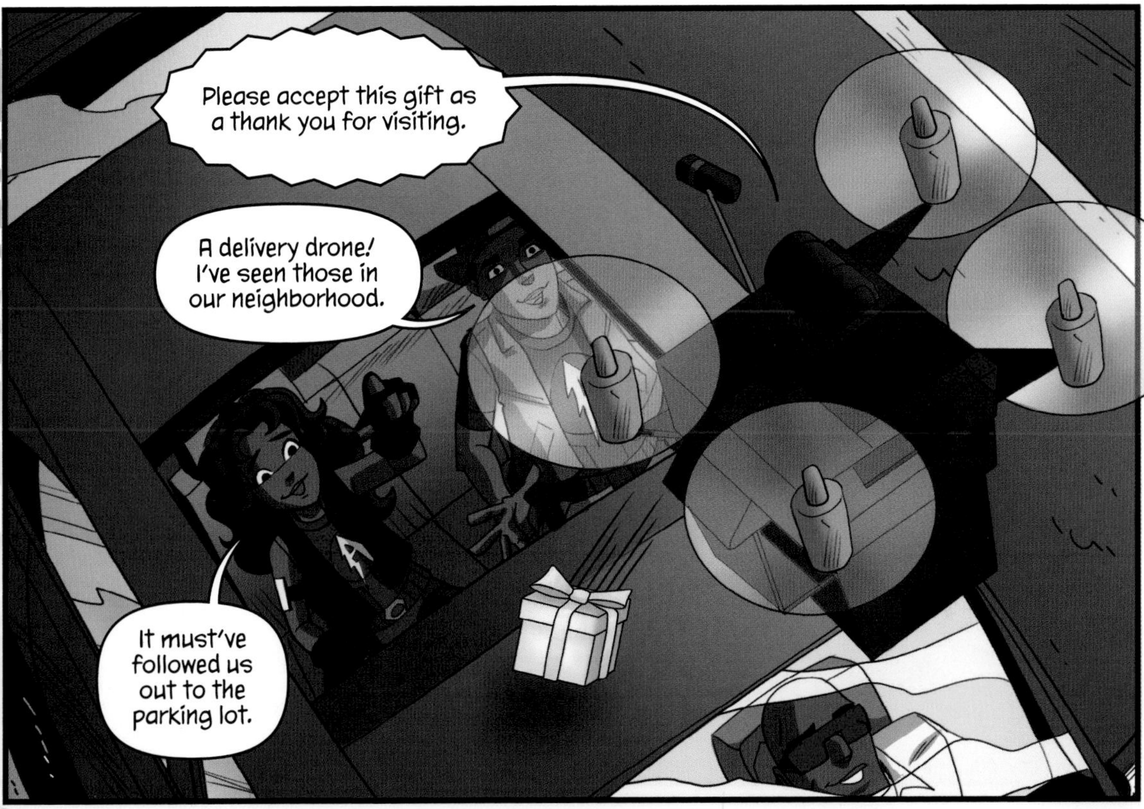
Please accept this gift as a thank you for visiting.
A delivery drone! I've seen those in our neighborhood.
It must've followed us out to the parking lot.

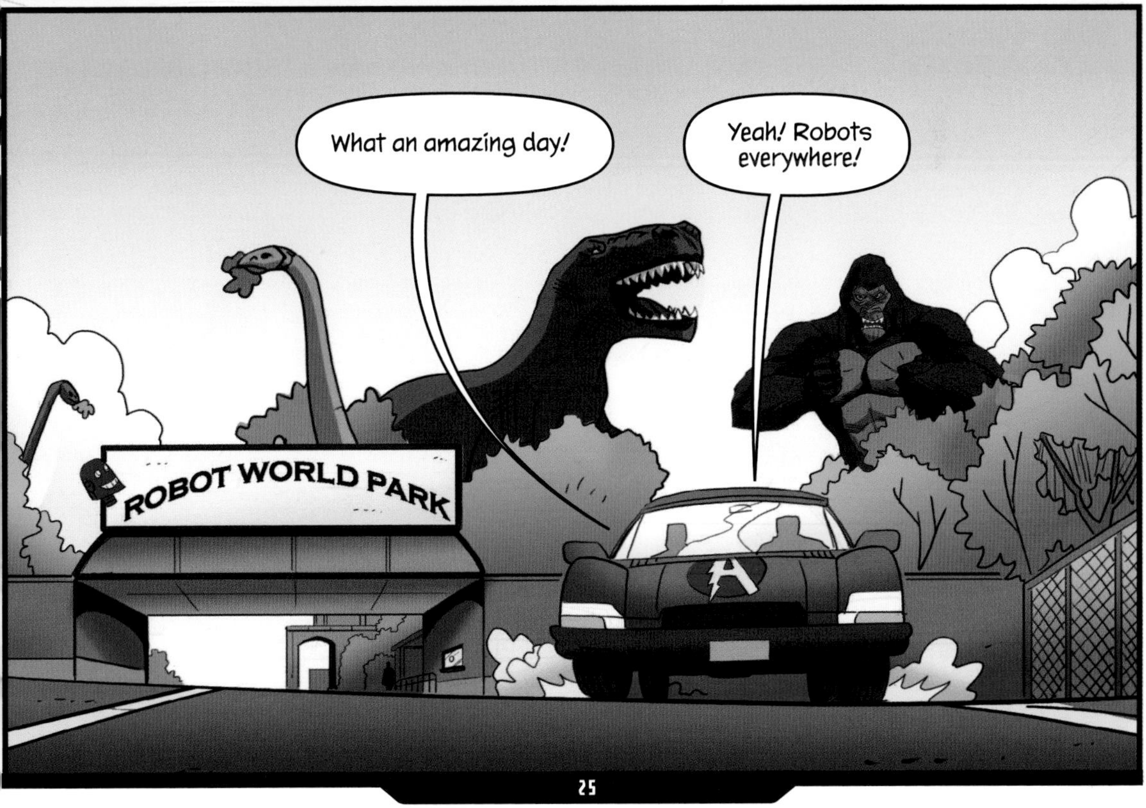
What an amazing day!
Yeah! Robots everywhere!
ROBOT WORLD PARK

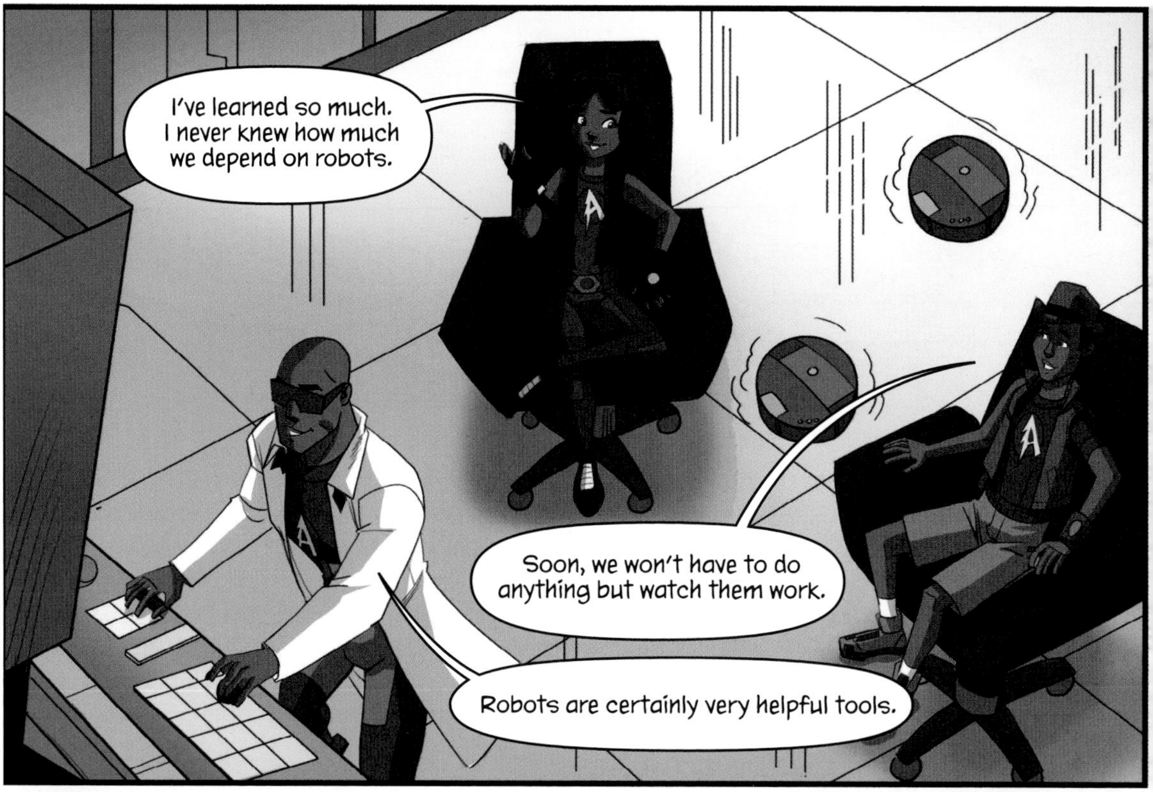
I've learned so much. I never knew how much we depend on robots.
Soon, we won't have to do anything but watch them work.
Robots are certainly very helpful tools.

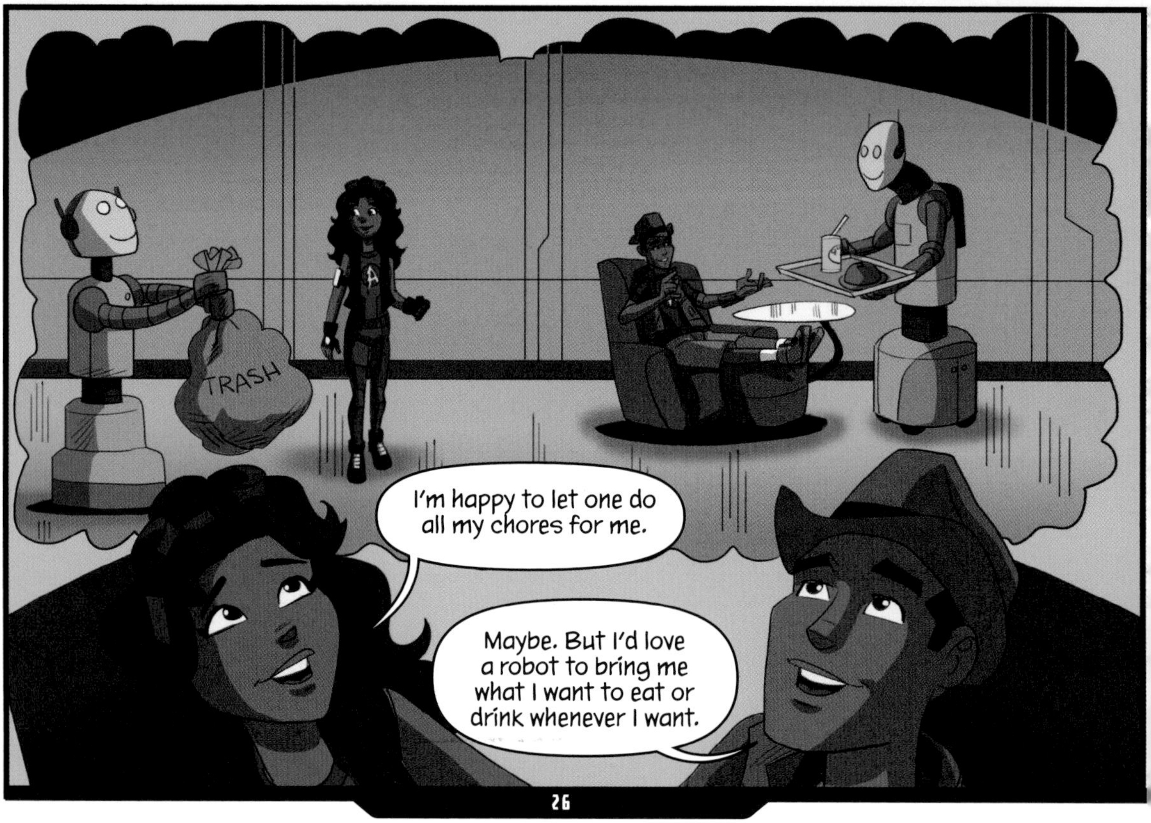
TRASH
I'm happy to let one do all my chores for me.
Maybe. But I'd love a robot to bring me what I want to eat or drink whenever I want.

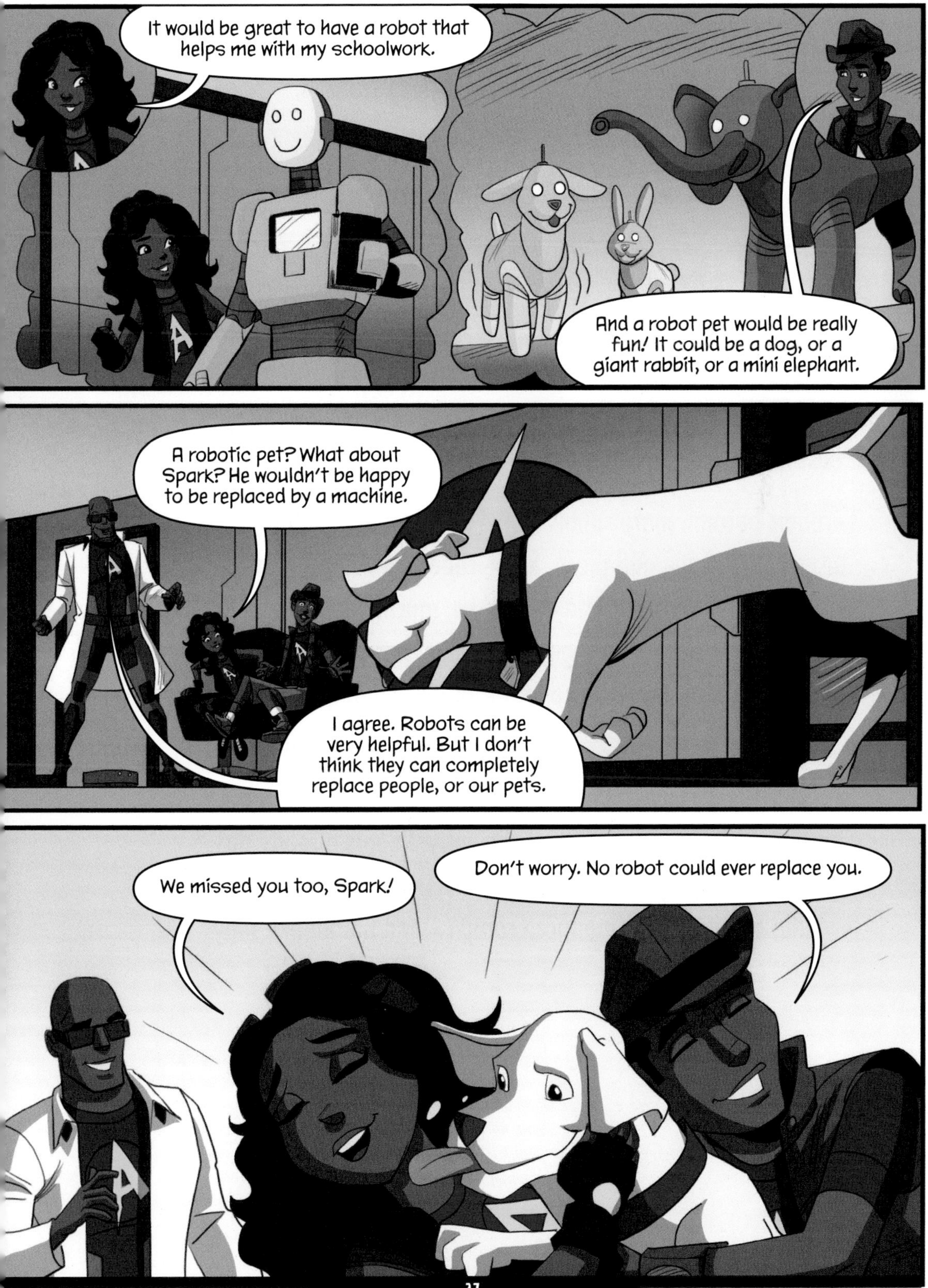
It would be great to have a robot that helps me with my schoolwork.
And a robot pet would be really fun! It could be a dog, or a giant rabbit, or a mini elephant.
A robotic pet? What about Spark? He wouldn't be happy to be replaced by a machine.
I agree. Robots can be very helpful. But I don't think they can completely replace people, or our pets.
We missed you too, Spark!
Don't worry. No robot could ever replace you.

WILL ROBOTS REPLACE HUMANS?

There are a lot of movies about robots. Some of these robots are friendly while others are dangerous. Robots in some films want to destroy humans. But in other movies robots work with people to save the world. Will robots ever be as smart and humanlike as we see in the movies? Could you someday have a best friend who's a robot? Maybe.

As robots become more sophisticated, they could have all the senses people have and more. Some robots can smell, taste, feel, see, and hear the world around us, much like people do. But robots can also be stronger and faster than humans. They can have artificial intelligence, or AI, to learn and grow.

Does this mean that humans could one day be replaced by robots? Probably not. It's likely that robots will keep working with humans to do things more efficiently. Robots already do repetitive and dangerous jobs for humans. But some people fear that as robots become more complex and humanlike they could take over.

British scientist Stephen Hawking worried about how quickly AI is being developed. He believed that the technology could do a lot of good if it's carefully controlled. But he thought that if robots learned to think for themselves, they could outgrow their human creators. He felt that rules are needed for how AI is used, so that people stay safe.

Technology and AI are moving at a fast pace, and the future looks exciting. Will robots be a help or a danger to humanity? What do you think?

GLOSSARY

allergic (uh-LUHR-jik)—when a person's body has a strong reaction to something, such as animal hair, a bee sting, or certain foods

android (AN-droyd)—a robot that looks and acts very similarly to a human being

animatronic (an-uh-muh-TRON-ik)—when a figure is animated and moves with the use of mechanical devices

artificial intelligence (ar-ti-FISH-uhl in-TEL-uh-juhnss)—the ability of a machine to think and learn like a person

automation (aw-tuh-MAY-shuhn)—the use of machines to do work without input from a person

diagnose (dy-ig-NOHS)—to find the cause of a problem or illness

domestic (duh-MES-tik)—relating to the household or family

exoskeleton (ek-soh-SKE-luh-tuhn)—a device worn on the outside of the body to provide support and strength

hazardous waste (HAZ-ur-duhss WAYST)—dangerous or poisonous materials that need to be disposed of safely

humanoid (HYOO-muh-noid)—humanlike in shape and appearance

mobility (moh-BIH-luh-tee)—the ability to move quickly and easily

roboticist (roh-BOT-uh-sist)—a scientist who studies and works in the field of robotics

terrain (tuh-RAYN)—the surface of the land

READ MORE

Leavitt, Amie Jane. *Dream Jobs if You Like Robots*. North Mankato, MN: Capstone, 2021.

Lepora, Dr. Nathan. *Robots*. New York: DK Publishing, 2018.

Williams, Dinah. *Robots*. New York: Starry Forrest Books, Inc., 2021.

INTERNET SITES

All About Robots
kidsdiscover.com/teacherresources/all-about-robots/

Robot Facts for Kids
kids.kiddle.co/Robot

Why Do We Send Robots to Space?
spaceplace.nasa.gov/space-robots/en/

ABOUT THE AUTHOR

Ailynn Collins has written several nonfiction children's books about amazing people, space, and science. Ailynn also loves to write fiction, especially stories about aliens, ghosts, witches, dinosaurs, and traveling through the universe. She lives outside Seattle, Washington, with her husband and five dogs.

ABOUT THE ILLUSTRATOR

Passionate comic book artist Eduardo Garcia works from his studio (Red Wolf Studio) in Mexico City with the help of his talented son, Sebastian Iñaki. He has brought his talent, pencils, and colors to varied projects for many titles and publishers such as Scooby-Doo (DC Comics), Spiderman Family (Marvel), Flash Gordon (Aberdeen), and Speed Racer (IDW).